THE

NEW-METHOD SPELLER

BASED UPON THE

LATEST REVISION OF WEBSTER'S INTERNATIONAL
DICTIONARY, ARRANGED IN ACCORDANCE
WITH THE LAWS OF ASSOCIATION,

AND

SPECIALLY DESIGNED TO MEET THE DEMAND FROM
THE CONSTANTLY INCREASING NUMBER OF
TEACHERS WHO BELIEVE THAT
SPELLING SHOULD BE

SYSTEMATICALLY TAUGHT

AS WELL AS PERFUNCTORILY HEARD.

———

"The one idea no sooner comes into the understanding than its
associate appears with it."—LOCKE.
"Words must owe their powers to association."—JOHNSON.

SEVENTIETH THOUSAND.

BALTIMORE:
SADLER-ROWE COMPANY,
PUBLISHERS.

INTRODUCTION.

A LETTER written by an individual is a valuable factor in determining his adaptability to business.

If the letter is incorrectly arranged, it indicates a want of acquaintance with accepted business forms; if the writing is bad, it shows that the accounts which he would be called upon to render would not be presentable; but if the *spelling* is bad, it at once *decides* the question of desirability against the applicant.

In England it is reported that at a recent examination of candidates for Public Service, nineteen-twentieths of the class failed in spelling, and an Educational Report of that country says: "Spelling is not what it should be. What we want is to *teach* spelling, and not merely to practise spelling."

Civil Service examination papers in this country also show a remarkable deficiency in this important study.

Correct spelling is, therefore, a requisite which evidently cannot be obtained by the old spelling methods. The situation requires a text-book by which spelling may be *taught*, and this educational demand is met by the *New-Method Speller.*

It is claimed for this text-book that its methods of presentation not only produce better results than can be obtained by any other means, but that by its use the Teacher is aided in the exercise of his own individual aptness in English instruction.

In the preparation of this work, the latest edition of Webster's International Dictionary has been taken as the standard.

SUGGESTIONS TO TEACHERS.

THE words of the *New-Method Speller* are arranged in accordance with the laws of association.

The primitive word, which is printed in **broad-faced** type, forms a key to the meaning of each derivative word which follows it, and the student is assisted further by having the primitive word divided into syllables and furnished with its proper accent. To reap the full benefit of this book, each recitation should be a combination of oral and written work. The primitive word should be pronounced and explained by the teacher, and a student required to state orally all of its given derivatives. Other students should express the various modifications of the primitive, in form and meaning, when combined with its several prefixes and suffixes. The class should then be required to write such words as the teacher may select. Original investigation by students may be cultivated by encouraging them to supply additional derivative words, which the prefix and suffix tables, with the rules of spelling, enable them to form.

Students, by this method, learn the correct pronunciation and meaning of primitive and derivative words, obtain a knowledge of the different elemental parts of words and of the ideas which they represent, and thus acquire the ability to use words intelligently both in speaking and writing.

iv

CONTENTS.

EXPLANATION.

A cross (+) represents so much of the primitive word as is printed in heavy type, and a star (*) represents the entire word; thus, if the primitive word be **profound,** *ly would represent *profound*ly and +ity, *profund*ity.

The distance of the star (*) from the remainder of the derivative will show how the word should be written, whether solid or with an intervening space; thus, if the primitive be **life,** *like, *-preserver, * insurance, would respectively represent *life*like, *life*-preserver, *life* insurance.

The accent of the primitive should be retained on the same syllable of each of its following derivatives, except when the derivative is enclosed within curves ( ), as shown in the first line of LESSON XLVI.

An indented line refers to the primitive of the preceding line, as illustrated in the eighth line of LESSON XXXIV.

PARALLELS (||) are used to indicate that in the following derivatives the primitive is used with a different meaning, as exhibited in the fifth line of LESSON XLIII.

vi

THE
NEW-METHOD SPELLER.

LESSON I.

gay; *ety, *eties, *ly.
page; +ing, ‖ *antry.
pare; *d, +ing, apple *r.
roast; *ed, *ing ear.
sam′ple; *s, *r, *d, +ing.
sat′in; *y, (*et′), (+een′).
see; *r, *n, *ing, un*n.
tack; *ed, *ing, *s.
veil; *ed, *ing, *s, un*.
vel′vet; *y, (*een′).
vend; *or, (*ee′).
wal′nut; English *, black *.

zeal; *ous, *ously, *ot.
ebb; *ed, *ing, * tide.
jog; *ged, *ging, * trot.
meal; *y, *iness, ‖ *time.
or′der; *ed, *ing, *ly.
paint; *ed, *ing, *er.
ward; *en, *robe, *s.
youth; *ful, *fulness.
an nex′; *ed, *ing, (*a′tion).
can′cel; *ed,*ing, (*la′tion).
dain′ty; +ies, +ily, +iness.
ear′ly; +ier, +iest, +iness.

LESSON II.

gaud′y; +ily, +iness, +ery.
jam; *med, *ming.
lash; *ed, *ing, *es, whip*.
meat; mince *, sweet*.
meet; *ings, *inghouse.
plaid; *ed, * muslin.
route; *s, (+ine′).
scorch; *ed, *ing.
soft; *er, *est, *en, *ness.
tank; *ard, water *, *s.
tool; *s, * chest.
val′id; (*ity), in*ate.

ash; *es, * pan, *-colored.
drawl; *ed, *ing, *ingly.
droop; *ed, *ing, *s, +ped.
glide; *d, +ing, +ingly.
hatch; *ed, *es, *way.
help; *er, *less, *mate.
hem; *med, *ming, *stitch.
i′tem; *ize, *ized, *s.
join; *ed, *ing, *er, *t.
keen; *ly, *ness, *er, *est.
kin′dle; *d, +ing, en*, en*d.
kitch′en; * garden, *maid.

1

LESSON III.

load; *ed, *ing, +en.
mat; *ted, *ting, door *.
raze; *d, +ing, +or.
wait; *ed, *ing, *er.
wet; *ter, *test, * nurse.
couch; *ed, *es, ac*ement.
jar; *red, *ring, a*.
last; *ed, *ing, *er, shoe *.
reap; *ed, *ing, *er.
sag; *ged, *ging.
scoop; *ed, * net.
seek; *er, *ing.
tap; *ped, heel*, *s.
de fer'; *red, *ring, (*ence).
deft; *ly, *ness.

in cur'; *red, *ring, *sion.
knock; *ed, *ing, *s, *er.
lull; *ed, *aby.
queer; *ly, *ness.
risk; *ed, *y, *s.
re'cent; *ly, *ness.
wharf; +ves, *age.
cheap; *ness, *er, *est.
call; *ed, *er, un*ed.
en grave'; *d, *r, +ing.
en tire'; *ly, *ty.
fa tigue'; *d, * dress.
grate; *d, *r.
hoe; *d, *ing, *cake.
in dict'; *ed, *ment.

LESSON IV.

net; *ting, *work, fishing *.
per fume'; *d, *ry, *r.
shirt; *ing, night*.
ci gar'; *s, (*ette').
daugh'ter; *-in-law.
feed; +d, *ing.
har'ness; *ed, un*.
jel'ly; +ies, +ied.
man'ner; *s, *ism, un*ly.
map; *ped, *ping.
oc cur'; *red, *ring, *rence.
prof'fer; *ed, *ing.
show'er; *y, * bath.
shrink; +unk, *ing, *age.
de fault'; *ing,*er(+ca'tion).

groove; *d, +ing.
hull; *ed, *er.
hus'tle; *d, +ing, *r.
or'phan; *s, *age.
ped'dle; *d, *r, +ing.
pick'le; *s, +ing, *r.
pie; *s, * crust, mince *.
prowl; *ed, *ing, *er.
rap; *ped, *ping, rip*.
huge; *ly, *ness.
inch; *es, two-* cable.
quaint; *ly, *ness, ac*.
screen; *ed, *ings, *s.
soot; *y, *iness.
tar'nish; *ing, un*ed.

LESSON V.

tart; *ly, *ness.
throb; *bed, *bing.
vi′o let; *s, *-colored.
ax′is; +le, +letree.
buck′et; *ful, fire *.
bun′dle; *s, *d, +ing.
car′pen ter; *s, +y.
col′lege; *s, (+iate, +ian).
dif′fi cult; *y, *ies.
dil′i gent; *ly, +ce.
grav′el; *ed, *ing, *ly.
hire; *d, +ing, *ling.
lace; *d, +ing, un*d.
lei′sure; *d, *ly.
mes′sage; *s, +enger.

nice; *ly, *ty, *ties.
par′ent; *s, (*al).
road; *s, *ster, rail*
scarce; *r, *st, +ity.
scat′ter; *ed, *ing.
scratch; *ed, *er, *es.
te′di ous; *ly, *ness, +um.
thrill; *ed, *ing, *s.
wreath; *s, *e, *ing.
wrist; *band, *let.
co′gent; *ly, +cy.
dun; *ned, *ning.
en grave′; *d, *n, +ì .
ex tol′; *led, *ling.
graft; *ed, *ing, en*.

LESSON VI.

mil′li ner; *y, man *.
im plant′; *ed, *ing.
in′stinct; (*ive, *ively).
joc′und; *ly, (*ity).
mulch; *ed, *ing.
pa′tient; *ly, *s, +ce.
prop; *ping, un*ped.
re frain′; *ed, *ing, ‖ *s.
vig′il; *ant, *ance.
bri′er; *y, * root, sweet*.
cru′el; *ly, *ty, *ties.
cuff; *ed, *ing, *s.
dot; *ting, un*ted, *s.
earn; *ings, un*ed.
hur′ry; *ing, +iedly.

par′son; *s, *age.
shud′der; *ed, *ing.
shock; *ed, *ingly.
sly; *ly, *ness, +ier.
wil′low; *y, weeping *.
can′o py; +ied, +ies.
hurl; *ed, *ing, *er.
noon; *day, *-flower.
owe; *d, +ing, *s.
peb′ble; *s, +y, *stone.
bile; +ious, +iousness.
brack′et; *s, * light.
ceil; *ed, *ing.
fol′low; *ed, *ing, *er.
lee; *ward, * shore, * rail

LESSON VII.

less; *en, *er, +st, +ast.
trav'el; *ed, *ing, *er.
av'er age; *d, +ing, *s.
chis'el; *ed, *ing, cold *.
gal'ler y; +ies, picture *.
loam; *s, *y, * mold.
lu'di crous; *ly, *ness.
pe'ri od; *s, (*ic, *ical).
rough; *er, *ness, *ly.
wedge; *d, +ing, *-shaped.
com mence'; *d, +ing.
el'e ment; (*al, *ary), *s.
in sult'; *ed, *ing, *ingly.
scent; *ed, *ing, *less.
sneak; *ed, *ing, *ingly.

war'ble; *d, +ing, *r.
weap'on; *s, *less.
yearn; *ed, *ing, *s.
in ure'; *d, +ing, *ment.
sap; *ped, *ping, *per.
e clipse'; *d, +ing, *s.
fes toon'; *ed, *ing, (+ival).
ob scure'; *ly, +ity.
smoth'er; *ed, *ing.
sneer; *ed, *ingly, *er.
tar'ry; +ied, *ing.
ab scond'; *ed, *er, *ing.
clam; *my, *miness, *bake.
fet'ter; *ed, *ing, *s.
glit'ter; *ed, *ing, *ingly.

LESSON VIII.

jock'ey; *s, horse-*, *ing.
la'zy; +ier, +iest, +iness.
loll; *ed, *ing, *ingly.
pre'cious; *ly, *ness.
pros'trate; *d, (+ion).
sec'tion; *al, +gment, bi+ct.
ap par'el; *ed, *ing.
balk; *y, *ed, *ish.
dif'fi dent; *ly, +ce.
doc'ile; (+ity, in+ity).
di vine'; *ly, +ity.
ef ful'gent; *ly, +cy.
gyp'sy; +ies, *ism.
in'voice; *d, +ing, *s.
mac'er ate; *d, +ing,(+ion).

pro fuse'; *ly, *ness.
reck'on; *ed, *ing, *er.
ad dict'; *ed, *ing.
ca ress'; *ing, *ingly, *es.
con ceit'; *ed, *edly.
de tach'; *ed, *ment.
fa ce'tious; *ly, *ness.
fa cil'i ty; +ies, +ate.
fall; *ing, down*en, *s.
grab; *bed, *bing, * bag.
gro'cer;; *y, *ies, green*.
ped'al; +estal, (+es'trian).
lac'er ate; *d, +ing, (+ion).
lame; *ly, *ness, *r, *st.
lath'er; *ed, *ing.

LESSON IX.

pose; *d, +ing, im*.
re cite′; *d, +al, (+a′tion).
as cribe′; *d, +ing, *s.
as sert′; *ed, *ing, *ion.
as sure′; *d, +ing, +ance.
bois′ter ous; *ly, *ness.
cur′tain; *ed, *ing, *s.
cu′ti cle; (+a′neous). ·
e ma′ci ate; *d, (+ion).
hoax; *ed, *ing, *er.
hob′by; +ies, * horse.
hol′low; *ness, *-hearted.
in′do lent; *ly, +ce.
in ert′; *ly, *ness, *ia.
lat′tice; *work, * window.

mar; *red, *ring.
plump; *er, *ly, *ness.
av′a rice; (+ious, +iously).
bul′le tin; *s, * board.
car′go; *es, super*.
dem′o crat; (*ic), (+cy).
de mure′; *ly, *ness.
e late′; *d, *dly, +ion.
groan; *ed, *ing, *s.
greed; *y, *iness, *ier.
pro found′; *ly, +ity.
quack; *s, *ery.
bi′cy cle; +ing, +ist.
chair; *manship, arm*.
im pair′; *ed, *ing, *ment.

LESSON X.

auc′tion; (*eer′, *eer′ed).
loi′ter; *ed, *ing, *er.
oc ca′sion; *ed, *ally, *s.
o′dor; *ous, *less, *ant.
reap; *ed, *ing, *er.
sham; *med, *ming, pillow *.
sip; *ped, *ping, *s.
tow′el; *ing, *s.
tres′pass; *ed, *ing, *er.
a ban′don; *ed, *ing, *ment.
ab bre′vi ate; *d, +ing.
con spic′u ous; *ly, *ness.
de bate′; *d, +ing, *r, +able.
glance; *d, +ing, +ingly, *s.
gen′er ous; *ly, +ity, un*.

in′fant; *ile, +cy, (*icide).
li′on; *ize, *-hearted, sea *.
lu′cid; *ly, (*ity), pel*.
mis′cel la ny; (+eously).
mi′ser; *ly, *y, *able, *ably.
mist; *ed, *ing, *y, *iness.
re hearse′; *d, +ing, +al.
re sort′; *ed, *ing, *s.
ap pren′tice; +ing, *ship.
chim′ney; *s, *sweep.
choir; +us, +al, +ister, *s.
con sult′; *ed, (*a′tion).
del′e ble; in+ible.
de lir′i um; +ous, +ously.
de vise′; *d. +ing, +or, (*e′).

LESSON XI.

fra′grant; *ly, +ce.
freight; *ed, * agent, +aught.
hei′nous; *ly, *ness.
hedge; *d, +ing, *row, *bog.
in iq′ui ty; +ies, +ous.
lump; *ed, *y, +nch.
nor′mal; *ly, * school.
out′rage; *s, (*ous, *ously).
re mem′ber; *ed, +ance.
scrawl; *ed, *ing, *er, *y.
scream; *ed, *ing, *s.
stamp; *ed, *ing, postage *.
a bridge′; *d, +ing, +ment.
ab′ro gate; *d, +ing(+ion).
bal′us ter; *ed, *s, +ade.

ca dav′er ous; *ly, *ness.
ca det′; *s, *ship, naval *.
ca lam′i ty; +ies, +ous.
ca jole′; *d, +ing, *ry.
dance; *d, +cing, (+sense′).
ec cen′tric; (*ity, *ities).
ec cle′si ast; (*ic, *ical).
fab′ric; *ate, (*a′tion).
gag; *ged, *ging, * rein.
ham′mer; *ed, *ing, *s.
pad′dle; *d, +ing, * wheel.
pail; *s, *ful, *fuls.
rack; *ed, *ing, *-rent.
you; *r, *rself, *rselves.
ab′sent; (*ed, *ing), (*ee′).

LESSON XII.

carp; *ed, *ing, *er.
cause; *d, +ing, *less, be*.
chafe; *s, *d, +ing dish.
chance; *s, *d, per*, mis*.
chant; *ed, *s, en*ment.
del′e gate; *d, +ing, (+ion).
delve; *d, +ing, *r.
harm; *ful, *less, un*ed.
leg′i ble; il*, (+il′ity).
log′ic; *al, il*al, (*ian).
bap tize′; *d, +zing, +st.
de cant′; *ed, *ing, *er.
farce; +ical, +ically.
fas′ci nate;*d, +ing,(+ion).
gar′ner; *ed, *ing, un*ed.

heav′en;*ward,*ly-minded.
im′be cile; *s, (+ity).
im bibe′; *d, +ing, *r.
man′a cle; *d, +ing, *s.
na′ked; *ly, *ness, * eye.
nose; *gay, +zzle, +stril.
ob′vi ate; *d, + ous, +ously.
palm; *istry, *y, (*etto).
pam′phlet; *s, (*eer′).
pan; *ned, *ning, *s, frying *·
ram′ble; *d, +ing, *r, *s.
rich; *er, *est, *ly, *ness, *es.
ta′per; *ed, *ing, *ingly, *↳
a′mia ble; +ly(+il′ity),un*.
broach; *ed, *ing, -un*ed.

LESSON XIII.

broil; *ed, *ing, *er, em*.
brook; *let, *s.
chest; * founder, broad-*ed.
chide; *d, +ing, +den.
chink; *ed, *ing, *y, *s.
chock; *ed, *ing, *ablock.
churl; *ish, *ishly, *ishness.
de coy'; *ed, *ing, *-duck.
ded'i cate; *d, +or, (+ion).
de fect'; *ive, +iciency.
de file'; *d, +ing, *ment.
ed'i fy; +ied, (+ica'tion).
forge; *d, +ing, *r, *ry.
frame; *d, *work, * house.
gen'u ine; *ly, *ness.

glow; *ed, *ing, *worm.
her'e sy; +tic, (+t'ical).
im'mi nent; *ly, +ce.
im mure'; *d, +ing, *ment.
mag'ic; *al, *ally, (*ian).
mag'is trate; (+nan'imous).
ni'ter; +ate, +ic, +ogen.
ob struct'; *ed, *ing, *ion.
plat; *ted, *ting, *s.
rein; *ed, *ing, check *.
sedge; *d, +y, * wren.
ab'sti nence; (+e'mious).
ab surd'; *ly, *ity, *ities.
brush; *ed, *ing, *es, hair*.
buff; *ed, *ing, *er, (*et').

LESSON XIV.

bulk; *ed, *ing, *y, *iness.
coax; *ed, *ing, *ingly.
coil; *ed, *ing, *s, re*, un*.
dash; *ed, *ing, *y, *board.
de fray'; *ed, *ing, *ment.
e lim'i nate; +ing, (+ion).
e lon'gate; *d, +ing,(+ion).
flaunt; *ed, *ing, *ingly.
flay; *ed, *ing, *er.
flinch; *ed, *ing, un*ingly.
harp; *ed, *ing, *er, auto*.
ob lique'; *ly, *ness, +ity.
rav'age; *d, +ing, *r, *s.
sa'vor; *ed, *ing, *y, *less.
a'gent; +cy, +cies, co+cy.

ag'gra vate; *d, (+ion).
ca nal'; *s, * boat, * lock.
can'non; *ade, * ball.
can'on; *ize, *ized, (*icals).
de lin'quent; +ce, +cy, *s.
de mand'; *ed, *ing, *able.
em'blem; (*at'ic, *at'ical).
e mend'; *ed,*ing,(*a'tion).
fa nat'ic; *al, *ism, *s.
fa'ther; *ly, *land, un*ly.
fath'om; *ed, *ing, un*able.
glis'ten; *ed, *ing, +er.
hate; *d, +ing, *ful, *fulness.
ha'zel; *ly, *nut, witch *.
haz'ard; *ed, *ing, *ously.

LESSON XV.

man'date; +tory, (+mus).
o'di um; +ous, +ously.
on ; *set, *ward, *-looker.
par'si mo ny; +iously.
sect; (*a'rian, *a'rianism).
source; *s, re*, re*s, re*less.
team ; *s, *ster, *ing, *work.
tu i'tion ; *ary, in*, (in+ve).
whis'ky; +ies, * barrel.
woo ; *ed, *ing, *er, un*ed.
burst; *ing, out*, cloud-*.
cough; *ed, whooping *.
de mean' ; *ed, *ing, *or.
de mol'ish; *ed, (+tion).
e merge'; *d, +ing, +ence.

em'i grate; *d, (+tion).
em'i nence; *s, +cy, +t.
e mo'tion ; *s, *al, *alism.
em'u late; *d, +ing, +or.
feign; *ed, *ing, *er, +t.
fel'low ; *ship, *-creature.
fel'on; *y, (*ious, *iously).
fi'nal;*ly, +ish,+ite,(in+ite).
in'dus try; +ies, (+ious).
in fat'u ate; *d, (+ion).
in fect'; *ed, *ious, *ion.
in sert'; *ed, *ing, *ion.
in sid'i ous; *ly, *ness.
lec'ture; *d, +ing, +er, *s.
leg'a cy; +cies, (+tee').

LESSON XVI.

loy'al; *ly, *ist, *ty, dis*.
man'gle; *d, +ing, +er, *s.
ma'jor ; (*ity), * general.
numb; *ed, *ing, *ness, be*.
plan; *ned, *ning, *ner, *s.
a cute'; *ly, *ness,+ly,+ness.
ap plaud'; *ed, *ing, +se.
ap pre'ci ate; *d, (+ion).
ar raign'; *ed, *ing, *ment.
car'i ca ture; *d, +ist, *s.
cell; *ar, *ular, *uloid, *s.
chill; *ed, *ing, *y, +blain.
chol'er; *ic, *ine, *a morbus.
ci'pher; *ed,*ing,de*,de*ed.
cir'cle; +uit, +ling, +ulate.

de o'dor ize; *d, +ing, +er.
de range'; *d, +ing, *ment.
der'o gate; (+ion), (+ory).
en gross'; *ed, *ing, *ment.
en hance'; *d, +ing, *ment.
en roll'; *ed, *ing, *ment.
en'ter prise; *s, +ing.
en vel'op; *ing, (*e, *es).
en vi'ron ; *ed, *ing, *ment.
e quip'; *ped, *ping, (*age).
ex ist'; *ed, *ing, *ence, pre*.
ex te'ri or; *s, +nal, +nally.
fin'ger; *ed, *ing, * reading.
first; *ly, *-class, twenty-*.
fleet; *ly, *ness, *er, *-footed.

LESSON XVII.

foul; *ness, *-mouthed, * ball.
fre'quent; *ly, +cy, in*ly.
fret; *ted, *ting, *ful, *work.
fur'nish; *ing, *er, +ture.
in cep'tion; +eptive, +ipient.
in vert'; *ed, +se, +sion.
mouth; *ful, *fuls, *piece.
mow; *ed, *ing, *n, lawn *er.
muff; *ed, *ing, *le, *ler, *s.
musk; *y, *rat, *iness.
must; *y, *iness, *ier, *ard.
pre scribe'; *d, +ption.
pro scribe'; *d, +ptive.
ri'fle; *d, breech-loading *.
scene; *s, *ry, *shifter, +ic.

straw; *berry, *-colored.
a'gue; +ish, *s, * fit.
arc'tic; *s, * circle, ant*.
as sas'sin; *ate, (*a'tion).
ax'i om; *s, (*at'ically).
close; *r, *st, *ly, *ness.
cold; *er, *est, *ly, *-blooded.
com'bat; *ed, *ive, *ant.
com bine'; *d, (+a'tion).
com'ment; *ed, *ary, *ator.
com'pa ny; +ies, (+ions).
com'pli cate; *d, (+ion).
com ply'; +ied, *ing, +iance.
com pute'; *d, +ing, +able.
con cede'; +ssive, +ssions.

LESSON XVIII.

con cern'; *ing, un*ed.
cook; *ed, *ing stove, *book.
con struct'; *ed, *ion, +e.
con sume'; +able, +ption.
con verse; (+ant),(+a'tion).
con vict'; *ed, *ing, *ion.
crit'ic; *al, *ally, *ise, *ism.
de pre'ci ate; +ive, (+ion).
dew; *y, *berry, *drop.
di vorce'; *d, *able, *ment.
do'nate; *d, (+or, +ion).
due; *bill, +ty, un+tiful.
es teem'; *ed, (+imable).
ex hib'it; *ed, *or, (*ion).
ex pect'; un*ed, (*a'tion).

ex pe'ri ence; +iment, +t.
ex plain'; +atory,(+a'tion).
ex port'; *ed, *er, (*a'tion).
ex tem'po re; (+a'neous).
ex tend'; *ed, +sive, +sion.
ex ter'mi nate; +or(+ion).
floor; *ed, *ing, *walker, *s.
force; +ing, +ible, reen*, *s.
fric'tion; *al, *less, * balls.
fruit; *age, *ful, *less, *tree.
fun; *ny, *nier, *niest.
an tic'i pate; *d, (+ion).
an'ces tor; +ess, (+al), +y.
a ris'to crat; (*ic), (+cy).
bell; *-shaped, dinner *, *s.

LESSON XIX.

belle; *s, *s-lettres, +aux.
bu'ry; +ied, *ing, +ial.
ca'ter; *ed, *ing, *er, *ess.
chief; *tain, * justice.
com'fort; *ed, *er, un*able.
com mend'; *able,(*a'tion).
com men'su rate; +ble.
com mode'; +ity, (ac+ate).
com pact'; *ed, *ing, ‖ (*s).
com'pend; (*ium, *ious).
com pile'; *d, +er, (+a'tion).
com prise'; *d, +ing, *s.
clip; *ped, *ping, *per, *pers.
coach; *ing, *es, *man, * dog.
co erce'; +ing, +ive, +ion.

coop; *ed, *ing, *er, *erage.
det'ri ment; (*al), (+tion).
de vest'; *ed, *ing, [law].
dig'ni fy; +fied,+tary,+ty.
dim; *med, *ming, *ly, *ness.
di vest'; *ed, *ing, *iture.
dor'mant; +er window.
dredge; +er, +ing machine.
dumb; *ness, *-bell, +my.
emp'ty; +ier, +iness.
en am'el; *ed, *er, * paper.
en croach'; *ing, *ment.
e rect'; *ed, *ing, *ion, *ness.
flip; *ped,*pant,*pancy,*per.
fraud; *ulent, *ulently, de*.

LESSON XX.

pre vent'; *ed, *ive, *able.
price; *d, +ing, *less, * list.
prim; *med, *ming, *ness.
sue; +ing, +it, en*, en+ing.
throne; de*, de*d, de+ing.
cloud; *y, *ier, *iest, *less.
con jec'ture; +ing, +al, *s.
con'se crate; +ing, (+ion).
con'se quence; *s, (+tial).
con'tra ry; (+ily, +iness).
con'tro ver sy; +t, +tible.
con va lesce'; +ent, +ing.
con viv'i al; *ly, (*ity).
con voke'; +king,(+ca'tion).
con vulse'; *d, +ing, +ion.

crock; *s, *ery, ‖ *ed, *ing.
crook; *ed, *ing, *edness.
crude; *r, *st, *ly, +ity.
moth'er; *ly, *less, *-in-law.
mu'cus; +ous, +ilage.
mut'ton; *y, * chop.
path; *less, *way, *s.
pa'thos; (+et'ic),(+ol'ogy).
punch; *ed, *eon, * pliers.
rav'el; *ed, *ing, un*.
re trieve'; *d, +er, +able.
rob; *ber, *bery, *bing.
rope; +y, *-walk, * ladder.
rise; +ing, +er, +en.
rogue; +ery, +ish, *s.

LESSON XXI.

shave; *r, *d, +ing brush.
sheep; *ish, *fold, *-headed.
steel; *ing, *yard, * mill.
stern; *ly, *ness, ‖ * wheel.
spur; *red, *ring, *s.
trick; *y, *ish, *ster, *ed, *s.
tric'kle; *s, *d, +ling.
trip; *pingly, * hammer.
trite; *ly, *ness, (+ura'tion).
tri'umph; *ed, *ing, (*ant).
trou'ble; *d, +ing, *some.
tru'ant; *ly, +cy, *s.
trudge; *s, *d, +ing.
um'brage; (*ous, +el'la).
ur'ban; (*ity, *e), sub*.

vac'cine; +ate, (+a'tion).
vac'il late; *d, +ing, (+ion).
vo ra'cious; *ly, (+ty).
voy'age; +ing, *s, (+eur').
caus'tic; *al, *ally, +terize.
char'ter; *ing, * member.
chron'ic; *al, *le, *ler.
col lide'; *d, +ding, +sion.
de fi'cient; *ly, +cy, +cies.
de prave'; *d, +ing, +ity.
ear'nest; *ness, * money.
fag; *ged, brain *, *-end.
gal'lon; *s, standard *.
harsh; *er, *est, *ly, *ness.
her met'ic; *al, *ally.

LESSON XXII.

ig nite'; +ing, +ible, +ion.
in'du rate; +ing, (+ion).
in vid'i ous; *ly, *ness.
lus'ter; +ous, il+ious.
lynch; *ed, *ing, * law.
main tain'; *ing, (+enance).
mange; +y, +iness, +ier.
ma nip'u late; +ing, +or.
mash; *ed, *ing, *y, * vat.
mask; *ed, *er, *s, +querade.
mas'ti cate; +ing, (+ion).
mes'mer ize; +izing, +ism.
mi'grate; *d, +ing, e*, im*.
mor'al; *ist, (*ity), (*é).
mor'tal; *ly, (*ity), +gage.

mill; *er, * pond, ‖ *s, *ion
mim'ic; *ked, *king, *ry, *s
mir'a cle; *s, (+ulously).
mirth; *fulness, *less.
mis'sile; +ve, +on, +onary.
mit'i gate; +ing, (+ion)
ob'du rate; *ly, +cy.
pal'ace; *s, +tial, * car.
pan'ic; *s, *-stricken.
prof'fer; *ed, *ing, *s.
pro'gramme; *s, * music.
scaf'fold; *ed, *ing, *s.
scald; *ed, *ing, *s, * head.
tap'es try; +ies, * carpet.
teem; *s, *ed, *ing, *less.

LESSON XXIII.

af fin'i ty; +ive, chemical *.
an'nal; *s, *ist, (*is'tic).
awk'ward; *ly, *ness.
ba na'na; *s, * bird.
ca tarrh'; *al, (*ine).
mood; *ily, *iness, +e, +el.
mon'u ment; *al, *s.
mold; *ed, *ing, *er, *s.
mo lest'; *ed, *ing, (*a'tion).
mourn; *ed, *ing, *ful.
mur'der; *ous, *ously, *er.
mus'ter; *ed, *ing, * roll.
mu'ta ble; (im+bil'ity).
mu'ti late; *d, +ing, (+ion).
mut'ter; *ed, *ing, *ings.

mu'tu al; *ly, (*ity).
muz'zle; *d, +ing, *s.
myth; *ic, *ical, (*ol'ogy).
chal'lenge; *d, +ing, *s.
cher'ish; *es, *ed, *ing, *er.
clamp; *ed, *ing, *s, * nail.
clan; *nish, *nishness, *s.
code; +ify, +ifier, +icil.
con cil'i ate; +ing, (ion).
con clude'; *d, +ding, +sion.
con nive'; *d, +ing, +ance.
con'sti tute; *d, (+ent).
cow; *boy, *catcher, *hide.
coy; *ly, *ish, *ishness.
craft; *ily, *iness, *sman.

LESSON XXIV.

cube; *d, +ing, +ic, +ical.
cul'mi nate; +ing, (+ion).
cul'pa ble; *ness, +rit.
cun'ning; *ly, *ness.
curb; *ed, *ing, *s, * bit.
curd; *le, *led, *ling, *y.
cus'to dy; (+ian, +ians).
des'ic cate; *d, +or, (+ion).
des'o late; *ly, (+ion).
det'o nate; +or, (+ion).
dev'as tate; +ing, (+ion).
de vote'; *d, +ing, +ion, (*e').
di min'ish; un*ed, +utive.
dom'i nate; (+eer', +a'tion).
dow'er; *less, en+ed.

du'el; *ing, *ist, *s.
e lude'; *d, +ding, +sion.
em bel'lish; *ing, *ment.
e ter'nal; *ly, *ist, +ity.
e van'gel; *ize, *ized, *ist.
ex hort'; *ing, *er, (*a'tion).
ex'i gence; +cy, +cies, +t.
ex'pe dite; (+ent), (+tion).
ex pos'tu late; *d, +ing.
foil; *ed, *ing, *s, ‖ tin *.
grow; *s, *ing, *n, *th.
per vade'; *d, +ersely, +ert.
ridge; +y, *band, *pole, *s.
sound; *ing, (+o'rous, +a'ta).
ve ra'cious; (+ify, +itable).

LESSON XXV.

apt; *ly, *ness, *itude, in*, in*ly, in*itude, ad*able.

car; *s, horse *, drawing-room *, sleeping *, freight *, *ry, *ried, *riage, *rier, *ryail, *t, *twright, * coupler.

col'o ny; +ies, +ize, +ized, (+iza'tion), +ist, +ists, (+ial).

fire; +ing, *side, *proof, *board, *works, * alarm, * insurance.

flow'er; *ing, *y, *pot, *ing plants, *s, +id, (+id'ity).

gauge; *d, +ing, *able, +er, steam *, rain *, printer's *.

hack; *ed, *ing, *er, *s, * saw, || *s, *ney, *man.

hair; *y, *brush, *dresser, *breadth, *splitting, horse*.

hail; *ed, *ing, *stone, *storm, *shot, *-fellow.

in; *ner, *ning, *most, *come, *wardly, *truder, here*.

ink; *ed, *ing, *y, *iness, *stand, black *, printer's *.

la'bor; *ed, *ing, *er, *-saving, *atory, (*ious, *iously).

lath; *ed, *ing, *s, * nail, *-shaped, * brick, *work.

lit'i gate; +ating, +ant, (+a'tion), (+ious, +iously, +iousness).

maid; *s, *en, *enly, *servant, house*, milk*.

neigh'bor; *s, *ly, *ing, *hood, *liness, un*ly.

oak; *en, *s, black *, chestnut *, poison *, * bucket.

pad; *ded, *ding, un*ded, *s, * cloth, *dle, *dling, *dle wheel.

rail; *ed, *ing, *s, *road, *roading, * fence, elevated *way.

LESSON XXVI.

safe; *ly, *guard, *ty lamp, *-keeping, +ve, +vior, *s.

sal'u ta ry; (+u'brious, +ute'), (+uta'tion), +vage, (+va'tion).

salt; *ing, *y, *iness, +ary, +eratus, *peter, *cellar, * water.

sauce; *pan, +y, +ily, +iness, +ier, +iest, +er, apple *.

saw; *ed, *ing, *dust, *mill, *-set, *fish, *horse, *yer, hand*.

ta'ble; *cloth, *-land, *spoon, *ware, turn*, *t, *s.

test; *ed, *ing, *s, * tube, * paper, *y, *ily, *iness.

wag'on; *s, (*ette'), *er, *ful, *load, four-horse *.

waist; *band, *cloth, long *ed, short *ed, *coating.

year; *ly, *book, *ling, fiscal *, leap *, civil *, off *.
job; *s, *ber, *bing, *bery, *bing house, * printer.
key; *s, *board, *hole, *note, *stone, *ed, *ing, * wrench.
kiln; *-dry, *-dried, *-drying, *s, brick*, lime*, glaze *.
knee; *s, * joint, *-deep, *-high, *pan, knock-*.
law; *s, *yer, * book, *maker, *-abiding, by-*.
ab **hor´;** *red, *ring, *rence, *rent, +rid, +ror.
⟩ed; *ding, *stead, *post, *room, *clothes, spring *.
bev´el; *ed, *ing, * gear, * wheel, * angle, * square.
ca´ble; *d, +ing, * road, telegraphic *, *gram, *s.
cal´i co; *es, *back, * bass, * printing, shirting *.

LESSON XXVII.

dig; *ged, *ging, *ger, *gings, *ger wasp.
ear; *ache, *drop, *ring, *mark, *shot.
ease; +y, +y-chair, +y-going, +ily, un+iness, dis*.
egg; *ed, *ing, *plant, * beater, *-shaped, *shell.
end; *ed, *ing, *less, *ways, fag-*, un*ing.
fan; *ned, *ning, * wheel, *ning machine.
fly; *ing, +ew, +own, +ier, * leaf, * wheel, * net, * catcher,
  *-bitten, * paper, house *, butter*, fire*, horse*, dragon *.
fog; *gy, *giness, * horn, be*, be*ged, petti*ger.
gas; *es, *sy, *eous, *-burner, * meter, * stove.
glad; *ly, *some, *den, *der, *dest, *dening.
half; *hose, *-witted, *-mast, +ve, +ved, +ving, +ves.
hang; *ed, *ing, *bird, *nail, *er-on, bell *er, *man.
har´bor; *ed, *ing, *less, *age, * master, *s.
hard; *er, *en, *-earned, *ness, *ware, *ly, case*ened.
i´dle; +er, +est, +y, +ing, *ness, *-headed, * wheel.
ill; *y, *ness, *-will, *-natured, *-timed, *-mannered.
keep; +t, *ing, *er, *sake, house*er, house*ing, un+t.
land; *lord, *lady, *scape, *mark, up*, low*, high*.
lap; *ped, *ping, * joint, *weld, *stone, *dog, ‖ *s.

LESSON XXVIII.

man; *ly, *kind, *liness, *ager, fisher*, fire*.

match; *ed, *ing, *es, * box, * game, over*ed.

o mit′; *ted, *ting, +ssion, +ssions, +ssive.

pack; *ed, *ing, un*, *age, *ages, *et, * horse.

pale; +er, *ness, *-faced, *-colored, +lor, +lid.

pound; *ed, *ing, *s, *er, * cake, *keeper, im*, im*ed.

pump; *ed, *ing, *s, air *, steam *, chain *, * stock.

sea; *sick, *going, *shore, * level, * lion, *man.

seam; *ed, *ing, *less, *stress, *stresses, *s, * presser.

se′cret; *ly,*ness, +cy, (*′e, *ive, *ion),*s,*ary, private *ary.

se lect′; *ed, *ing, *ion, *ive, *man, natural *ion.

tan; *ned, *ning, *ner, *nery, * bark, *-colored, *yard.

tar′dy; +ier, +iest, +ily, +iness.

ul′cer; *ate, *ated, *ating, *ous, (*a′tion), *s.

way; *side, *laid, * bill, * station, (high*, by*, water*, rail*).

ad ver tise′; *d, +ing, +er, (*ment, *ments).

blame; *d, +ing, +able, *less, *lessness, *worthy, un+able.

breath; *e, *ing, *lessly, *lessness, *ing place.

de′cent; *ly, +cy, +.cies, in*, in*ly, in+cy, in+cies.

eat; *ing, *er, *able, *en, +dible, (+dibil′ity), *ing house.

LESSON XXIX.

feath′er; *ed, *ing, *less, *-edge, * weight, * bed.

fill; *ed, *ing, *s, *er, ful*, ful*ment, re*, re*ed, re*ing.

game; *d, +ing, *some, *ster, +bler, +bling, back′+mon.

gar′nish; *ed, *ing, *ment, *er, (*ee′), un*ed.

gate; *way, *post, *man, *house, *less, * money.

gloss; *ed, *ing, *y, *iness, *ier, *iest, ‖ *ary.

hap′py; +ily, +iness, +ier, +iest, un*, un+ily, un+iness.

i de′a; *s, *l, *lism, *list, (*l′ity), *lize, *lized, *lizing.

i′dol; *ize, *ized, *izing, (*atry, *ater, *atress), *izer.

i o'*ta*; j+, j+ted, j+ting, j+tings, j+s, j+ter.

mar'ket; *ing, *able, *ableness, * garden, * wagon, * place.

na'tion; *al, *alize, *alist, (*al'ity), de*alize, de*alized.

off; *hand, *set, *shoot, *spring, *cut, (cut-*), *side.

pond; *s, * lily, *fish, *weed, mill *, ice *.

pok*e*; *d, +ing, *r, *weed, *bag, * bonnet.

pik*e*; *d, +ing, turn*, * pole, * perch.

quot*e*; *d, +ing, *r, +able, (+a'tion), mis*, mis*d, mis+ing.

roar; *ed, *ing, *ingly, up*, up*ious, up*iously.

rough; *ed, *ing, *en, *ly, *hew, *-grained, *shod, || *s.

sash; *ed, *ing, *es, || French *, vertical *, door *, window *.

LESSON XXX.

shak*e*; +ing, +ings, +en, +y, +ier, +iest, un*n, +er, +eress.

tr*ead*; +od, +odden, *ing, *mill, *le, *wheel.

ut'*ter*; *ed, *ing, *ance, *able, +most, *ly, un*able.

ware; *house, *room, *s, iron*, glass*, hard*, tin*.

warm; *ed, *ing, *er, *est, *ly, *th, *ing-pan, *-hearted.

watch; *ing, *ful, *man, *word, *maker, * guard, * night.

wo'man; *ly, *like, *hood, *ish, *kind, washer*, char*.

ac cept'; *ed, *ing, *ance, *able, (*abil'ity), un*able.

ac cess'; *ary, *ory, *ories, *ion, *ible, (*ibil'ity), in*ible.

an tag'o niz*e*; *d, +izing, +ist, +ists, +ism, (+is'tic).

beam; *ed, *ing, *s, *y, moon*, sun*, || * engine.

bus'*y*; +ily, +iness, +inesslike, +ier, +iest, *body, *bo ies.

but; *ted, *ting, a*, a*ted, a*ting, a*ment.

but'ter; *y, *ine, *man, *milk, *cup, *fly, apple .

can'd*y*; +ied, *ing, +ies, *like, *tuft, * syrup, sugar *.

chat; *ted, *ting, *ty, *tiness, *tering, *terbox, chit*.

chees*e*; +y, +iness, *monger, *paring, * press, * cake.

ev'er; *green, (*last'ing, *last'ingly, *more'), *glade, for*.

e'vil; * eye, *-eyed, *-minded, *-mindedness, *ness, * doer.

fish; *ing rod, *bait, *ery, *eries, *erman, *es, rock*, cod*, cat*.

LESSON XXXI.

flood; *ed, *ing, * gate, * tide, * mark, *s.
glass; *es, *y, *ware, *work, *house, cut *, eye*, +zier, * cutter.
latch; *ed, *ing, un*, un*ed, un*ing, *key, *string.
lev'el; *ed, *ing, *er, *ness, un*, spirit *, air *.
mas'ter; *ed, *ing, *y, * workman, harbor *, school*.
ma ture'; *d, +ing, *ly, +ity, +er, +est, im*, im*ly.
May; * Day, * pole, * queen, * flower, *ing.
nerve; *d, +ing, *less, +ous, +ously, *-shaken, un*d.
nest; *s, *le, *ful, *ling, *lings, * egg, bird's *.
object'; *ed, *ing, *ion, *ionable, un*ionable, un*ionableness
pass; *ed, *ing, *able, *ably, * book, im*able, *age.
quit; *ted, *ting, *claim, ac*, ac*ted, ac*ting, ac*tal.
rain; *ed, *ing, *fall, *bow, *drop, * water, *-tight.
sad'dle; *d, +ing, un*, *r, *bags, * horse, +ery.
sa pon'i fy; +ified, +ifier, (+ifica'tion), (+a'ceous).
search; *ed, *ing, * warrant, re*, re*es, un*able.
ship; *ped, *ping, *per, *ment, *builder, steam*.
take; +ing, +en, under*, under+ing, under+er, *-off, over*.
val'ue; *s, *less, +able, (+a'tion), in+able, in+ably.
waste; *d, *r, +ing, *ful, *fulness, *basket, * pipe, * gate.

LESSON XXXII.

weigh; *ed, *ing, *er, *master, *t, *ty, re*.
world; *ly, *liness, *ling, *ly-minded, *ly-wise, *-wide.
whip; *ped, *ping, *saw, *staff, *stick, horse*, *s.
yard; *s, *stick, *ful, *arm, ship*, steel*, farm*.
a gree'; *d, *ing, *able, *ably, dis*able, dis*ably.
ax; *es, *helve, *man, wood *, broad*, broad*es.
bag; *ged, *ging, *gage, *gage master, mail *, flour *.
boil; *ed, *ing, *ing spring, *er, *er iron, par*.
brake; *man, *s, * rubber, * wheel, air *, cane '.

2

can'd*le*; *s, *light, * power, electric *, (+ela'brum).
dea*d*; *en, *ly, *head, * center, +th, +thly, +thlike.
dent'*ist*; *ry, +al, +ifrice, (+i'tion). ‖ in+, (in+a'tion).
ea'gle; *t, *wood, *-eyed, *-winged, bald *, double *.
edg*e*; *d, +ing, *ways, * tool, * mill, wire *, *s.
el'e vat*e*; *s, *d, +ing, +or, (+ion), *d railway.
fad*e*; *d, +ing, *less, un*d, un+ing, un+ingly, un+able.
fail; *ed, *ing, *ure, +se, +lible, in+lible,(+libil'ity).
fame; +ed, +ous, +ously, *less, (in+ous, in+ously).
fam'i ly; +ies, (+iar, +iarly, +iarize, +iarized), (+iar'ity).
far; *ther, *thest, *fetched, *-stretched, *seeing, *sighted.

LESSON XXXIII.

farm; *s, *er, *ing, *house, *yard, stock *.
faith; *ful, *less, *fully, un*ful, un*fully, un*fulness.
gen't*le*; *man, *ness, +ly, *r, +ile, (+il'ity), un*ness.
hay; *stack, *loft, *mow, *rake, *-cutter, * press.
im prov*e'*; *d, +ing, *ment, +able, (+abil'ity), un*d.
im ply'; +ied, *ing, (+icate, +icated, +icating), (+ica'tion).
knit; *ted, *ting, *ting machine.
knot; *ted, *ting, *ty, *tiness, bow*, single *, double *.
lik*e*; *d, +ing, *ly, *lihood, *ness, un*, *-minded.
nee'dle; *s, *case, *woman, *work, *ful, *-pointed, darning *.
of'fice; *s, *r, *holder, post *, (+ial, +ious, +iate, +iated).
sai*nt*; *ly, *ed, +ctify, +ctified, +ctuary, *s.
sand; *y, *iness, *paper, * bag, * bed, * blast, *storm, * box.
san*e*; *ness, *ly, +ative, +ity, +itary, in*, in*ly, in+ity.
shar*e*; *d, *r, +ing, *s, *holder, *broker.
sharp; *ly, *ness, *-cut, *-witted, *shooter, *en, *er, *est.
shap*e*; *d, +ing, *r, *less, *ly, *lier, *liest, *liness, un*ly.
seed; *ed, *ing, *ling, *y, *less, *time, *sman, * corn, * oyster.
seiz*e*; *d, +ing, +ure, +able, .*r, dis*, dis*d, dis+ing.
tar; *red, *ring, *ry, *paulin, *water, c ɹl *, wood *.

LESSON XXXIV.

un'der ; *bid, *clothes, *current, *sign, *value, mis*stand.

walk ; *ed, *ing, *-over, *ing beam, floor*er, *ing stick, rope*.

web ; *bed, *bing, *worm, *-toed, cob*.

wind ; *fall, *gall, *storm, *mill, *-broken, whirl*.

ap'ple ; *s, * blossom, * dumpling, * tart, pine*, crab *.

bal'lot ; *ed, *ing, *s, *er, * box, * boxes.

case ; *d, + ing, *s, *ment, *harden, * knife, book*, un*, un*d,
   + ual, + ually, + ualty, + ualism, + uist, + uistic, + uistry.

catch ; + ught, *ing, *er, *es, *penny, *up, *word.

cheer ; *ed, *ing, *ful, *fully, *fulness, *ily, *y, *s.

de liv'er ; *ed, *ing, *y, *ies, *er, *ance, un*ed.

de pend' ; *ed, *ent, *ant, *ency, in*ent, in*ence.

en force' ; *d, + ing, *ment, re*, re + ing, re*ment.

fault ; *y, *less, *lessness, *-finding, *-finder, de*, (de + ca'tion).

fa'vor ; *ed, *ite, *itism, *able, un*able, dis*.

glut ; *ted, *ting, *s, *ton, *tonous, *tony, *tonish.

great ; *er, *est, *ly, *ness, *-hearted, *-grandfather, * seal.

hat ; *ter, *band, *bands, *box, * block.

hill ; *y, *iness, *ock, *side, *top, *s, up*, down*.

hon'or ; *able, *ary, *ably, + est, + esty, dis + esty, un*ed.

LESSON XXXV.

il lus'trate ; *d, + ating, + ious, + iously, (+ a'tion).

know ; + ew, *ing, *n, *ledge, ac*ledge, un*n.

lead ; *ed, *s, *en, * pencil, * color, black *, white *, red *.

le'ver ; *age, *s, * watch, * jack, canta*, compound *.

light ; *ed, *ing, *s, *house, *-ship, electric *, flash *.

one ; *ness, *self, *-sided, + ce, *-story, + ly.

pend ; *ing, *ency, *ent, *ant, *ulum, im*ing.

sheet ; *ed, *ing, *ings, *s, * iron, * anchor.

shoe ; *ing, + d, *black, *maker, * string, un + d, horse*.

slip; *ped, *ping, *knot, *per, *pery, *shod, *pery elm.
sure; *ly, *ty, *tyship, *ties, *-footed, in*, in+ance, unin*d.
sweet; *er, *ly, *en, *ness, *meat, *-scented, * potato.
tin; *ned, *ning, *ner, *man, *smith, * foil, block *.
troop; *ed, *ing, *er. ͡, * ship, *fowl, *bird.
tug; *ged, *ging, *s, *boat, * iron, * of war.
use; *d, *s. *ful, *fully, *fulness, *less, +ual, +urp, +ury.
u ten'sil; *s, (+il'ity), (+ilita'rian),(+ilize,+ilized,+ilizing).
win; *ned, *ning, *ner, *some, *someness, *ning post.
act; *ed, *ing, *or, *ion, *ive, re*, re*ion, en*, en*ment.
as sess'; *ed, *ing, *ment, *or, un*ed, re*ing, re*ment.

LESSON XXXVI.

as sign'; *ed, *ing, *ment, *able, (*ee', *or').
au'thor; *ize, *ized, (*ity, *ities), *s, un*ized, un*izing.
calm; *ed, *ing, *ly, *ness, be*, be*ed, be*ing.
char'i ty; +ies, +able, +ably, un+able, Sisters of ✶.
chick'en; *s, *-hearted, *-breasted, *pox, * cholera, +weed.
chip; *ped, *ping, *s, * ax, * bonnet, Saratoga *s.
chop; *ped, *ping, *s, *per, *py, *ping block, *-logic.
ci'ty; +ties, +tizen, +tizens, +vic, +vil, +vilize, un+vilized.
de pos'it; *ed, *ing, *or, *ory, +t, +se, (+si'tion), *s.
de sire'; +ing, +ous, +able, +ableness, un+able, un+ableness.
dif'fer; *ed, *ing, *ence, *ent, *ently, in*ence, in*ent.
em'pha sis; +size, +sized, (+t'ic, +t'ically, un+tic).
fat; *ter, *test, *ten, *tening, *ty, *ling, *ness, *s, soap *.
fear; *ed, *ing, *ful, *fully, *less, *fulness, *lessness.
feast; *ed, *ing, +al, +ival, (+iv'ity), love *.
fee'ble; *r, *st, +y, *ness, *-minded, en*d.
grease; *d, +ing, +y, +ily, +iness, *r.
heir; *ed, *ing, *s, *ess, *loom, *less, in+it, in+itance, disin+it.
hon'ey; *ed, *ing, *bee, *comb, *suckle, *moon, *-tongued.
im'age; *s, *ry, (+ine, +inative, +ina'tion).

LESSON XXXVII.

im pel'; *led, *ling, +ulse, +ulsive, +ulsion.
in trude'; *d, +ding, *r, +sive, +sion.
lamp; *light, *lighter, *black, arc *, * shade.
laugh; *ed, *ing, *able, *ter, *ingstock, *ing gas.
man'i fest; *ed, *ing, *ly, (*o), (*a'tion), un*ed, *a
man'u al; *ly, +facture, +factured, +facturer, +mit, +script.
near; *ed, *ing, *ly, *ness, *sighted, *-legged.
odd; *er, *est, *ity, *ly, *ness, *s, * Fellow.
pain; *ed, *ing, *ful, *fully, *fulness, *staking.
par'al lel; *ed, *ing, *s, (*ogram), * ruler, un*ed.
par'don; *ed, *ing, *able, *ableness, *ably, *er, un*able.
prompt; *ed, *ing, *ly, *er, *ness, im*u.
rot; *ted, *ting, *ten, *tenness, *ten stone, dry *, potato *.
run; +an, *ning, *ner, *away, *let, *ning gear, home *, out*.
shop; *ped, *ping, *per, *book, *keeper, *lifter, *girl, junk *.
shoot; *ing, *er, +gun, +-proof, + tower, *ing gallery.
shoul'der; *ed, *ing, * blade, * knot.
shrink; +unk, *ing, *ingly, un*ingly, *er, *age.
smoke; *d, +ing, *r, +y, *less, *stack, *-dry, +ing car.
tel'e graph; *ed, *ing, *er, *ic, +gram, +phone, +scope.

LESSON XXXVIII.

var'nish; *ed, *ing, *er, * tree, oil *, un*ed.
wealth; *y, *ier, *iest, *ily, common*.
black; *ened, *ing, lamp*, *smith, *mail, * lead.
bod'y; +ily, +ice, *guard, * servant, * snatcher, em*.
coast; *ed, *ing, *er, *wise, sea*, *ing trade.
cool; *ed, *ing, *ly, *er, *est, *ness, *-headed, +d.
com pose'; *d, +ing, +ure, *r, +itor, (+i'tion), (+t).
con fess'; *ed, *ing, *or, *ion, *ional.
con fide'; *d, +ing,*r, (+ant', +ante', +en'tial), (ence).

con vey'; *ed, *ing, *er, *ancer, *ancing, +oy, re*.
dec'o rate; *d, +ating, +ator, +ative, (a'tion), (+ously, +um).
dirt; *y, *ier, *iest, *ily, *iness, * bed.
eve; *ning, *ntide, Christmas *, Hallow+n.
e'ven; *ed, *ing, *ly, *ness, *handed, *-minded, un*.
e vent'; *s, *ful, *fulness, *ual, *ually, *uate, un*ful.
ex tract'; *ed, *ing, *or, *ion, (*s, fluid *).
field; *er, *work, * hand, * day, corn*, coal *.
flag; *ged, *ging, *man, *stone, * station, *staff, *ship.
girl; *ish, *ishness, *ishly, *hood, school*, school*s.
grass; *y, *plot, *hopper, *-grown, * land, blue *, +ze.

LESSON XXXIX.

hum; *med, *ming, *bug, *buggery, *drum, *ming bird.
in duce'; *d, +ing, *r, *ment, +ible, +t, +tion, super*.
jail; *ed, *ing, *er, * fever, * delivery, *s.
kiss; *ed, *ing, *er, *es.
kin; *dred, *ship, *d, *dly, *dness, *d-hearted, un*d.
lan'guish; *ed, *ing, *er, *ment, +or, +id, +idly, +idness.
loud; *er, *est, *ly, *ness, *-voiced, *-mouthed.
lum'ber; *ed, *ing, *er, *man, * room, * wagon.
mel'o dy; +ies, +ist, (+ious, +iously, +iousness, +eon).
men'tal; *ly, +ion, +ioned, +or, * arithmetic, un+ionable.
phys'ic; *al,(*ian), (+que'), (+og'nomy, +ol'ogy, +ol'ogist).
pick; *ed, *ing, *er, *ax, *pocket, *et guard. tooth*.
pro mote'; *s, *d, +ing, *r, +ive, +ion, +ions.
rec'og nize; +zed, +zable, (+tion), (+zance), (+zee', +zor').
rec om mend'; *ed, *ing, *er, *able, *ably, *atory.
sin cere'; *r, *st, *ly, in*ly, +ity, in*, in+ity.
sim'ple; *r, *st, +y, (+ic'ity), *ton, +ify, (+ifica'tion).
skip; *ped, *ping, *pingly, *per, *jack.
sky; +ies, *ey, *light, *rocket, *ward, *lark, *-high.
soap; *s, *y, *suds, * bubble, toilet *, (+on'ify), (+ona'ceous).

LESSON XL.

so'd*a*; * fountain, * water, cooking *, washing *, + ium, sal *.
tam*e*; *d, + ing, + able, *ness, *r, *st, un*d, un + able.
tempt; *ed, *ing, *ingly, *er, (*a'tion), at*ed, at*ing.
wel'com*e*; *d, + ing, *r, *ness, un*, un*ness.
wrin'kl*e*; *d, + ing, + y, *s, un*, un*d.
an'nu *al*; *ly, (+ ity, + ities, + itant), semi*ly.
an'swer; *ed, *ing, *er, *able, *ableness, un*able.
ag ri cul'tur*e*; + al, + ally, + alist, + alists.
bleach; *ed, *ing, *er, *ery, *ing powder, un*ed.
blea*k*; *er, *est, *ish, *ness, *ly, + ch, + ched, + ching.
bridg*e*; *d, + ing, *board, draw*, cantalever *.
con duc*e*'; + ing, + ible, + t, + ted, + ting, + tor, + tion, mis + t.
con fus*e*'; *d, + ing, + ion, *dly, un*d.
con'que*r*; *ed, *ing, *or, + st, + sts, un*able.
de clar*e*'; *d, + ing, + ative, + atory, (+ a'tion, + ations).
del'i *cate*; *ly, in*, + cacy, + cacies, + ght, + ghtful, + ghted.
e lec'tr*ic*; *al, + ify, + ified, + otype, + oplate, (*ian, *ity).
fin*e*; *d, + ing, + able, *s, ‖ + ly, + ness, *r, *st, * arts, re*.
f*i*nd; *ing, *er, *ings, + ound, + oundling, + oundlings.
gau*ze*; + y, + iness, wire *, cotton *.

LESSON XLI.

h*os'pice*; + st, + stess, + tel, + spital, + spitable, (+ spital'ity).
in flict'; *ed, *ing, *er, *ion, *ions, un*ed.
l*ong*; *er, *-armed, * clothes, (*ev'ity), + engthen, ‖ *ed, *ing.
min*ce*; *s, *d, + ing, + ingly, *r, *-meat, * pie.
mix; *ed, *ing, *er, *able, *ture, un*ed.
mo'ment; *ary, *arily, (*ous, *um), *ly, *s.
moon; *light, *lit, *stone, *beam, * face, *-faced.
need; *ed, *ing, *y, *ful, *fully, *less, *lessly.
ob tain'; *ed, *ing, *er, *able, un*ed, un*able.

or na*te'*; *ly,*ness, +mc it, un+mented, +mental, +mentation.
pall; *bearer, *iate, *iative, (*ia'tion), ap*ed, ap*ing.
pep'per; *ed, *ing, *y, *mint, *grass, * caster.
per mit'; *ted, *ting, +ssion, +ssive, +ssible, *s.
red; *der, *dest, *den, *dish, *bird, *-hot, * tape.
re tr*ea*t'; *ed, *ing, +ct, +cted, +ctive, +ctible, +ction.
re joice'; *s, *d, +ing, +ingly, *r, +ings.
scant; *y, *ly, *ness, *ily, *iness, *ier, *iest.
sel*f*; *ish, *ishly, *ishness, *-confidence, him*, them+ves.
shed; *ding, *der, *s, water*, wagon *, wood *.
smooth; *ed, *ing, *ly, *ness, *er, *est, *-faced.

LESSON XLII.

work; *ed, *ing, *house, *man, *ing-day, *ing classes, water*s
wri*te*; +ing, +ten, +ing school, type*r, under*r.
at tor'ney; *s, *ship, * at law, *-general.
au'to *graph*; +harp, +crat, +matic, +type.
a vail'; *ed, *ing, *able, (*abil'ity), un*able.
bee*f*; *steak, *y, *eater, * tea, +ves.
cof'fee; *man, *pot, *house, Java *, Rio *.
col lect'; *ed, *ing, *or, *ible, *orship, *ively, *ion.
dra*ft*; *ed, *ing, * horse, +ughtsman, +ughting room.
ex'er cise; *d, +ing, *r, *s, +able.
ex haust'; *ed, *ing, *less, *ive, in*ible, (in*ibil'ity).
ex p*el*'; *led, *ling, +ulsive, +ulsion, +ulsions.
ex press'; *ed, *ing, *age, *ible, *ion, * office.
fal*se*; *ly, *ness, *hood, +ify, +ity, (+et'to), *-faced.
glu*e*; *d, +ing, *y, +ten, +tinous, (ag+tina'tion), un*d.
ground; *ed, *ing, *less, *work, *nut, * rent, un*ed.
haugh'ty; +ily, +iness, +ier, +iest.
head; *ed, *ing, *er, *y, *ache, *land, *less, *strong, *s.
he'ro; *es, *ine, *ism, (*ic, *ical, *ically).
il lu*de*'; *d, +ding, +sively, +siveness, +sory, dis+sion.

LESSON XLIII.

judg*e*; *d, +ing, *ship, +ment, ad*, mis*.

ju di′*cious*; *ly, *ness, +ial, +iary, ad+ate, in*.

le*ase*; *d, *hold, *holder, +sor, (+see′), re*.

mar′r*y*; +ied, *ing, +iage, +iageable, un+ied, inter*.

mean; *ly, *ness, ‖ *time, *while, ‖ *ing, *t, ‖ *s.

neck; *band, *lace, *tie, *wear, * yoke, stiff-*ed.

night; *ly, *dress, *shirt, *time, *-eyed, * key.

nois*e*; *less, +y, +ily, +iness, +ier, +iest.

or′i gin; (*ate, *ated, *ating, *ator, *al, *ally).

oys′ter; *s, *ing, * bed, * dredge, * shell, pearl *.

pau′per; *ism, *ize, *ized, *izing, (*iza′tion), *s.

peg; *ged, *ging, *ger, *s, * top, shoe *.

queen; *ly, *liness, *-post, * bee, *'s ware, May *.

school; *boy, *house, *master, *-teacher, +ar, Sunday *.

tast*e*; *d, +ing, *less, +y, *ful, *fully, dis*ful, un*d.

th*ree*; *fold, *-cornered, +rice, +ird, +irty, +irtieth.

ab*le*; *r, *st, *-bodied, (+il′ity, +il′ities), dis*, un*.

at tach′; *ed, *ing, *ment, *able, (*e′), de+ed.

bur′glar; *y, (*ious, *iously), * alarm.

cl*ear*; *ly, *ness, *er, *est, *ance, *-headed, +ify.

LESSON XLIV.

clean; *er, *est, *ness, *ly, *se, *sed, un*.

cur′r*ent*; *ly, *ness, +ency, (+ic′ulum), re+ing, oc+ence.

cur′ry; +ied, *ing, +ier, *comb, *combs.

de scen*d*′; *ed, *ing, *ant, *ent, +t, con*, con+sion.

dens*e*; *ly, +ity, *r, *st, con*, con*r, (con+a′tion).

de port′; *ed, *ing, *ment, (*a′tion), im+, re+, sup+.

de spi*se*′; *d, +sing, +te′fully, (+cable, +cably).

dra′ma; *tize, *tized, *tizing, *tist, (*t′ic), melo*.

ey*e*; *d, +ing, *ball, *lash, *witness, *let, bull's-*.

fam'i ly; +ies, (+iarize, +iarized), (+iar'ity), (un+.ar).
fan'cy; +cied, *ing, +ciful, +cier, +ciest, (+tas'tic), * store.
fee; *d, *ing, * simple, +udal, +udalism, *s.
fit; ‗*ted, *ting, *ter, *test, un*ted, re*ted, ‖ *s, *ful.
fix; *ed, *ing, *ture, *tures, *ed light, gas *ture.
fla'vor; *ed, *ing, *less, *ous, un*ed, *s.
fresh; *ly, *ness, *er, *est, *en, *et, *man, re*ment.
gov'ern; *ed, *ing, *or, *ess, *ment, mis*, un*able.
gum; *med, *ming, *my, *boil, * wood, * elastic.
haste; *d, +ing, +en, +y, +ier, +iest, +ily, +y pudding.
hear; *d, *ing, *er, *say evidence, un*d, re*ing.

LESSON XLV.

here; *about, *by, *in, *after, *with, *tofore, *upon.
in'stant; *ly, (*a'neous, *a'neously), +ce, +ces, +ced, +cing.
li'a ble; (+il'ity, +il'ities, re+il'ity), re*, unre*.
li'bel; *ed, *ing, *er, *ous, *ously, *ant.
li'bra ry; +aries, (+a'rian, +a'rianship), (+et'to).
man'tle; *d, dis*d, *s, +uamaker, (+il'la), ‖ +el.
name; *d, +ing, *less, +able, *ly, *sake, mis*, sur*, Christian *.
oil; *ed, *ing, *er, *y, *iness, *cloth, * painting, cod-liver *.
pawn; *ed, *ing, *er, (*ee'), *broker, * ticket.
pearl; *y, *ash, *fish, * eye, *-eyed, * diver, *s.
pet'ty; +ily, +iness, +ier, +iest, +icoat, +ifoggery.
piece; *d, +ing, *meal, *work, * goods, *s, mouth*.
re peal'; *ed, *ing, *able, ap+, ap+ed, ap+ing.
re peat'; *ed, *ing, *er, *edly, (+i'tion), (+end').
ride; *s, +ing, +den, *r, *rless, +ing school, bed+den.
sea'son; *ed, *ing, *able, *ably, un*ed, un*able.
sec'ond; *ing, *ary, *arily, *-class, * hand, *hand clothing
se'ri ous; *ly, *ness, +-comic, +-comical.
serve; *d, +ing, +ant, +ice, +iceable, +ile, +itude, (+il'ity)
where; *by, *fore, +ever, *upon, *as, *at, *about.

LESSON XLVI.

ap peal'; *ed, *ing, *able, (+la'tion), (+lor', +lee').
cob'ble; *d, +ing, *r, *stone.
co here'; *d, +ing, +ence, +ent, in+ent, in+ence.
col'or; *ed, *ing, *less, *-blind, parti-*ed, dis*.
dis pense'; *d, +ing, *r, +able, +ary, (+a'tion), in+able.
fer'tile; +ize, +ized, (+ity, in+ity), in*.
fu'ture; *less, +ist, *s, * tense, (+ity, +ities).
gram'mar; (*ian, +t'ic, +t'ical, +t'icize), * school.
guar an tee'; *d, *ing, *s, (+y, +ies, +or).
guess; *ed, *ing, *ingly, *er, *es, *work.
guide; *d, +ing, +able, +ance, *book, *post, * bar.
har'mo ny; +ize, +ized, (+ious, +iously, +ic, +ica, +icon).
hoop; *ed, *ing, *er, * skirt, * iron, * tree.
hunt; *ed, *ing, *er, *sman, *ing lodge, fox-*ing.
husk; *ed, *ing, *y, *ing bee, ‖ *y, *ily, *iness.
in struct'; *ed, *ion, *or, *ress, (+ment), (+men'tal), un*ed.
in'tel lect; (*ual, *ually), (+igence, +igent, un+igible).
in trench'; *ed, *ing, *ment, un*ed.
i'ron; *ed, *ing, *smith, *ware, *-cased, cast *.
jump; *ed, *ing, *er, * seat, *-seat wagon, baby *er.

LESSON XLVII.

lin'en; +net, +seed, +sey-woolsey, * draper, (+o'leum).
man'age; *d, +ing, *able, *ment, *r, un*able.
note; *d, +ing, +ary, +ice, +ify, (+o'rious), (+ori'ety).
po lite'; *ly, *ness, im*, (+icy, +itics, +ish, un+ished).
pro pi'tious; *ly, +ate, +ator, +atory, (+a'tion), un*.
real; *ize, *ized, (*is'tic), (*iza'tion), * estate, un*.
sail; *ed, *ing, *er, *or, *boat, * loft, (top*, main*).
short; *en, *ening, *er, *est, ʍhand, *stop, *-waisted.
skill; *ed, *ful, *fully, *fulness, un*ed, un*ful.

tea; *spoon, *spoonfuls, *cup, * set, black *, green *.

teach; *es, *ing, *er, school-*er, school-*ing, +ught.

wax; *ed, *ing, *ed end, *y, *iness, * flower, bees*.

a bate'; *d, +ing, *ment, +able, *r, un*d.

ac com'mo date; *d, +ing, +or, (+ion), un*d, un+ing.

bril'liant; *ly, *ness, +ce, +cy, *s.

cler'gy; *man, +ic, +icalism, +k, +kship.

crys'tal; *line, *lize, *lized, (*liza'tion), *s, rock *.

cut; *ting, *ter, *lery, *worm, *-off, * glass.

de serve'; *d, +ing, +edly, +ingly, un*d.

do mes'tic; *ate, *ated, *ating, (+icile, +iciled).

LESSON XLVIII.

el'e gant; *ly, +ce, in*, in*ly, in+cy, in+cies.

free; *ly, *dom, *man, *dman, *mason, *-minded, * will.

freeze; *r, +eezing, +ozen, +ost, +ostbite, +ost-bitten.

gath'er; *ed, *ing, *er, *s, un*ed.

good; *ness, *ly, *-by, *-looking, *-natured, || dry *s.

hymn; *ed, *ing, *s, *al, *ology, * book.

im part'; *ed, *ing, *er, *ible, (*a'tion), un*ed.

im port'; *ed, *ing, *er, *ance, *ant, (*a'tion).

im pose'; *d, +ing, +ingly, +tor, (+i'tion), (+t), re*, re*d.

im press'; *ed, *ing, *ive, *ion, un*ed.

in'ci dent; *s, +ce, (*al, *ally), co*, co+ce.

jew'el; *ed, *ing, *er, *ry, *s, *er's gold.

learn; *ed, *ing, *er, *edly, un*, un*ed.

li'cense; *r, (*e'), *s, (+tiate, +tious), un*d.

lob'by; *ing, +ied, *ist, * member.

lo'cal; *ize, *ized, *izing, *ly, (*ity, *ities).

lock; *ed, *et, *jaw, *out, *-down, * stitch, pad*, un*.

mar'row; *y, *less, *bone, *fat, * squash.

mer'it; *ed, *ing, (*o'rious, *o'riously), de*, un*ed.

mer'ry; +ier, +iest, +ily, +iment, *-go-round.

LESSON XLIX.

melt; *ed, *ing, *er, un*ed, *ing point, s*ing.

na′ture; *s, +al, +ally, un+al, un+ally, ill-*d.

patch; *ed, *ing, *work, *y, *es, * ice.

pat′ent; *ed, *ing, (*ee′), *s, * office, un*ed.

pa trol′; *led, *ling, *man, *men, fire *.

plow; *ed, *ing, *point, *share, *boy, *man, un*ed.

pro ceed′; *ed, *ing, +dure, +ssion, (*s, +ss).

right; *ed, *ing, *ly, *ful, *eous, *-handed, un*eous, up*.

slaugh′ter; *ed, *ing, *er, *ous, *house, *man.

ac′cu rate; *ly, +cy, in*, in*ly, in+cy, in+cies.

ad mire′; *d, +ing, *r, (+able, +ably), (+a′tion), un*d.

ad mit′; *ted, *ting, *tedly, *tance, +ssible, +ssion.

a dore′; *d, +ing, +ingly, +able, +ableness, (+a′tion), un*d.

cal′cu late; *d, +ing, +or, +ive, (+ion), mis*, un*d.

chain; *ed, *ing, *less, *work, * pump, endless *, un*ed.

co ag′u late; *d, +ting, +tor, +ble, +tive, (+tion), un+ble.

coal; *y, +lier, +liery, *pit, *-black, * oil, * field.

co a lesce′; *d, +es′cing, *nce, *nt, +i′tion, +i′tionist.

de test′; *ed, *ing, *er, *able, *ably, (*a′tion).

de vel′op; *ed, *ing, *er, *able, *ment, un*ed.

LESSON L.

drug; *ged, *ging, *gist, *gists, *s, *get, *gets.

ed′it; *ed, *ing, *or, (*o′rial, *o′rially), (+i′tion, +i′tions).

e rase′; *d, +ing, *r, +able, +ure, *ment.

ex cuse′; *d, +ing, *r, +able, +ably, +ableness, *s, in+able.

fence; *d, +ing, *r, *less, worm *, rail *.

firm; *ly, *ness, *er, *est, *ament, in*ity.

gal′lant; *ly, *ry, (*ed, *ing), un*.

fer′ry; +ied, *ing, +iage, *man, *boat, * bridge.

gar′den; *ing, *er, * party, kitchen *, market *.

grade; *d, + ing, + ual, + ually, + uate, (+ ua'tion), (+ a'tion).
grain; *ed, *ing, ‖ + ary, + ge, + ule, + ulate, + ulated, + ite.
how ; *beit, *ever, *soever, some*, any*.
hu'man ; *ly, *ist, *ize, (*ity, *e', *e'ly, *e'ness), (*ita'rian)
hurt ; *ing, *ful, *fully, *fulness, un*, un*ful.
im'mi grate; *d, + ting, (+ tion), + nt, + nts.
in'sti gate; *d, + ing, + ingly, + or, (+ ion).
in sure'; *d, + ing, *r, + able, + ance policy, un*d.
juice; *less, + y, + ier, + iest, + iness, lemon *.
lodge; *d, + ing, *r, + ment, dis*, dis*d, dis + ment.
look ; *ed, *ing, *out, *er-on, *ing-glass, out*.

LESSON LI.

loft; *y, *ily, *iness, *ier, *iest, hay*, a*.
mar'ble; *d, + ing, *r, *ize, *-edged, *d paper, *s.
ob serve'; *d, + ing, *r, + able, + ance, + atory, (+ a'tion), un*d.
reach ; *ed, *ing, *less, *able, out*, over*.
sight ; *ed, *ing, *less, *ly, *liness, *-seeing, eye*, over*.
ap ply'; + ied, *ing, + iance, (+ icable, + icant), (+ ica'tion), mis*.
ap point'; *ed, *ing, *able, *er, (*ee'), *ment, + rtion, dis*.
ap proach'; *ed, *ing, *able, *ableness, un*able.
brand ; *ed, *ing, *er, *-new, *ing iron, fire*.
cease; *d, + ing, *less, *lessly, un + ingly, de*.
cer'tain ; *ly, *ty, + ify, + ified, (+ if'icate), un*.
de cay'; *ed, *ing, (+ id'uous, + id'uousness), un*ed.
de prive'; *d, + ing, *r, + able, (+ a'tion), un*d.
ev'i dent; *ly, + ce, + ced, + cing, State's + ce.
ex ceed'; *ed, *ing, *ingly, + ss, + ssive, + ssively.
ex cite'; *d, + ing, *r, + able, (+ abil'ity), *ment, + ant.
ex claim'; *ed, *ing, *er, + atory, (+ a'tion).
float; *ed, *ing, *er, *age, (+ a'tion, + il'la), + sam, a*.
fond ; *er, *est, *le, *ly, *ness, *ling.
fool ; *ed, *ing, *ery, *ishness, + ly, *'s cap, April *.

LESSON LII.

fra t*er'nal* ; *ly, + ernity, (+ ernize, + ricide, + ricidal).
gloom ; *y, *ily, *iness, *ier, *iest, *ing, + aming.
grace ; *d, + ing, *ful, un*ful, *fully, *less, + iously, scape*.
gross ; *ly, *ness, *er, *est, *-headed, * receipts, en*, en*ing.
grub ; *bed, *bing, *ber, *worm, * hoe, * ax, *s.
guilt ; *y, *ily, *iness, *less, *lessness, *-sick.
hag ; *ged, *ging, *gish, *gard, *gardly, + edge, + edges.
heed ; *ed, *ing, *less, *lessly, *lessness, un*ed.
hoarse ; *ly, *ness, *r, *st, *n.
ho'ly ; + ier, + iest, + ily, + iness, *day, + iday, un*.
in'ti ma*te* ; *d, + ting, *ly, + cy, (+ tion).
in tro duc*e'* ; *d, + ing, *r, + tive, + tion, + tory.
in vent' ; *ed, *ing, *or, *ress, *ive, *iveness, *ion, (*ory).
in vest' ; *ed, *ing, *or, *iture, *ment, un*ed.
in ves'ti gat*e* ; *s, *d, + ing, + ive, + or, (+ ion).
lop*e* ; *d, + ing, e*, e*d, ᵤ+ᵢng, e*r, e*ment.
o bey' ; *ed, *ing, + dience, + dient, + isance, dis*.
pro duc*e'* ; *d, + ing, *r, + tive, + tiveness, + tion, (+ t).
prom'is*e* ; *d, + ing, + er, + or,(+ ee'), + sory,(com'*, com'*d).
re ceiv*e'* ; *d, *r, + eipt, + ep'tacle, + ep'tion, + ip'ient, (+ ipe).

LESSON LIII.

san'gu*ine* ; *ly, + uinary, (+ aree', *-froid'), (con + uin'ity).
u'n*it* ; *y, + ion, (+ iver'sal, + an'imous), (*e', + ique').
va'por ; *y, *ous, *ize, (*if'ic, *iza'tion), * bath, (e*ate).
wis*e* ; *ly, + dom, *acre, *-hearted, || like*, no*, length*.
   wit ; *ty, *ticism, *tily, *tier, *tiest, *less, *ness, out*.
ac'id ; nitric *, (*ity, *ify, *ified, *ulate, *ulous), *s.
a pol'o g*y* ; + ies, + ist, + ize, + ized, (+ et'ic, + et'ical).
aw*e* ; *d, + ing, + ful, + fully, + fulness, *-struck, un*d.
Christ ; *en,*endom, *ian, *ianize, (*ian'ity),*mas, *mas tree.

dou'ble; *d, +ing, *ness, +y, *tree, *-minded, * entry, +oon.

doubt; *ing, *less, *ful, un*edly, +ious, in+itable.

dwell; +t, *ing, *er, *ing house, *ing place, in*ing.

en dure'; *d, +ing, +able, +ance, un+able.

en'ter; *ed, *ing, +ance, +ances, +y, +ies, (+ee').

en'vy; +ies, +ied, *ing, +ious, +iable, un+iable.

four; *th, *teen, +ty, +tieth, twenty-*, * hundred, *fold,
    *handed, *-cornered, *-in-hand, *-o'clock.

fore; *most, *man, *judge, *sight, *cast, *taste, *head,
    *noon, *ordain, *tell, *go, +th, +ward.

gen'er al; *ly, *ize, *ship, out*, major *, (*ity).

LESSON LIV.

hand; *y, *iness, *ily, *bill, *cuff, *ful, *icap, *some,
    *kerchief, *writing, *saw, * car, under*, off*, long*, short*.

ice; *d, +ing, +y, +iness, *berg, *bound, *-built, * cream

jaunt; *ed, *ing, *ing car, ‖ *i:y, *iness, *ier, *iest.

lag; *ged, *ging, *gingly, *gard.

late; *r, *st, *ly, *ness, +t'ter, +st, +stly, be*d.

leak; *ed, *ing, *age, *y, *iness, *ier, *iest, a*.

leap; *ed, *ing, *frog, *ing pole, * year.

ma te'ri al; *ism, *ist, *ly, *ize, (*iza'tion), im*.

neat; *er, *est, *ly, *ness, + weight, + profit.

ob lit'er ate; *d, +ing, +ive, (+ion).

oc'cu py; +ied, *ing, +ant, +ancy, (+a'tion), un+ied, pre*.

pass; *ed, *ing, *er, *able, *age, *enger, *word, im*able.

pas'sion; *ate, *ately, *less, dis*ate, +ive, +ively, im+ible.

per'il; *ous, *ously, *ousness, im*, im*ed, im*ing.

per'ish; *ed, *ing, *able, *ableness, im*able.

per'ma nent; *ly, +cy, +ce, im*.

per plex'; *es, *ed, *edly, *ing, *ity, un*ed.

per'se cute; *d, +ing, +or, (+ion, +ions), un*d.

que'ry; +ried, *ing, +rist, +st, +stion, un+stionable.

LESSON LV.

re sign'; *ed, *ing, *edly, (*a'tion), un*ed.

re spect'; *ed, *ing, *ful, *fully, *able, dis*, (+ ite, + ited).

si'lence; *d, + cing, + t, + tly, + t partner.

an nounce'; *d, *ment, *r, (+ ia'tion), un*d.

com mand'; *ed, *ing, *er, *ery, *ment, (*ant').

crumb; *le, *led, *ling, *ly, *cloth, * brush.

crust; *y, *ily, *iness, *ed, *ing, (*a'ceous), pie *.

de form'; *ed, *ing, *ity, *ities, (*a'tion), un*ed.

e lect'; *ed, *ing, *or, *ive, *ion, (*ioneer'), (+ igible), (+ ite').

en ter tain'; ed, *ing, *ingly, *er, *ment.

green; *er, *est, *ish, *ly, *ness, *grocer, *-eyed, Paris *.

horse; *manship, *fly, *shoe, *-radish, *-jockey, * car, saw*.

lime; *d, + ing, + y, *kiln, *water, *stone, * light, bird*.

lim'it; *ing, *less, *ed company, un*ed, (*a'tion, de*a'tion).

mi'nor; + us, + im, + imize, + imum, + uet, + ute, (*ity, + u'tia).

op'e ra; * glass, * house, *te, *ted, *ting, *tor, (*tion).

op por tune'; *ly, *ness, + ity, + ities, in*, in*ly.

plug; *ged, *ging, un*, un*ged, un*ging, fire *.

poi'son; *ed, *ing, *er, *ous, *ousness, * oak.

por'tion; *ed, *ing, *less, ap*ment, pro*, pro*ed, dispro*.

LESSON LVI.

quar'rel; *ed, *ing, *er, *some, *someness.

ran'cid; *ly, (*ity), + or, + orous, + orously.

re main'; *ed, *ing, *der, (+ ant, + ants).

thin; *ner, *nest, *ly, *ness, *-soled, *-skinned.

thor'ough; *ly, *ness, *fare, *going, *bred.

thirst; *y, *ier, *iest, *ily, *iness, *ed, *ing.

vic'tor; *y, (*ious, *iously, *iousness, *ia).

whale; *boat, *man, + er, + ing, *bone, * fishery, sperm *.

vo'cal; *ly, *ist, *ize, + ice (+ ca'tion, + cab'alary, + cif'erous).

an'chor; *ed, *ing, *age, *et, *-hold, sheet *.
damn; *able, +age, +ages, +aged, +aging, un+aged.
de fal'cate; *d, +ing, (+or), (+ion, +ions).
de feat'; *ed, *ing, +sible, +sance, in+sible.
es tab'lish; *ed, *ing, *er, *ment, *ments, dis*.
ex am'ine; *d, +ing, *r, (+a'tion), un*d.
grand; *ly, *ness, *er, *eur, (*il'oquence), *father, *son.
hinge; *d, +ing, *less, *s, * joint, un*, un*d.
hop; *ped, *ping, *per, *ple, *scotch, grass*per, ‖ *s, * vine.
in quire'; *d, +iring, +iry, *r, +is'itive, (+est).
leaf; *y, *let, *less, *iness, * bud, fly *, +ves.

LESSON LVII.

link; *ed, *ing, *work, * motion, un*, un*ed.
ma chine'; *ry, +ist, * gun, sewing *, (+ate), (+a'tion)
mor'al; *ly, *ize, *ized, *ist, de*ize, (*ity, im*ity).
mem'o ry; +ries, +ir, +rable, (+rial, im+rial), (+ran'dum)
num'ber; *ed, *ing, un*ed, out*, +ate, +ous, in+able
op pose'; *d, +ing, *r, (+ite, +itely), (+i'tion), un*d.
place; *d, +ing, *man, *-proud, dis*, dis*d, dis+ing, dis*ment.
post; *ed, *ing, *mark, *al card, *age stamp, * office, *er, im*.
rec'on cile; *d, +ing, +able, *r, ir+able, (+ia'tion).
re cov'er; *ed, *ing, *y, *able, ir*able, (+upera'tion).
re cruit'; *ed, *ing, *er, *ment, *s.
seal; *ed, *ing wax, * ring, great *, ‖ *s, *er, *-brown.
tech'nic; *al, *ally, (*al'ity, *al'ities), poly*.
al'ter; *ed, *ing, *able, (*a'tion), un*able, un*ably.
a mel'io rate; *d, +ing, +ive, (+ion).
com pare'; *d, +ing, +atively, +ison, (+able, in+ably).
de claim'; *ed, *ing, *er, +atory, (+a'tion, +a'tions).
de duce'; *d, +ing, +ive, +ible, +t, +ted, +ting, +tive, +tion.
dif fuse'; *d, +ing, *r, +ible, +ive, +iveness, +ion.
di gress'; *ed, *ing, *ive, *iveness, *ion.

LESSON LVIII.

gap ; *ped, *ping, *-toothed, ‖ *e, *ed, *ingstock, *eworm.

gold ; *en, *en-rod, *smith, *fish, *-beating, * leaf, * mine.

hy′dran*t* **;** +ogen, (+au′lic, +om′eter), (+opho′bia).

in tox′i cat*e* **;** *d, +ting, un+ting, +nt, (+tion).

in′tri ca*te* **;** *ly, +cacy, +cacies, (+gue, +guery).

in trin′sic ; *al, *ally, * value, * energy.

it′er ate **;** *d, +ing, +ive, (+ion, re+ion), re*, re*d.

li/e **;** *less, *boat, *like, *-size, *-preserver, * insurance, +ve,
+ved, +ving, +ver, +velihood, +vely, +velier, +ve stock.

lu′bric ; *ate, *ated, *ating, *ant, *ator, *al, (*a′tion), (*ity).

nar′row ; *ed, *ing, *ly, *ness, *-minded, * gauge.

ob scure′ ; *d, +ing, *ly, +ity, +ities, (+a′tion), un*d.

per pet′u at*e* **;** *d, +ating, +al, +ally, (+a′tion), (+ity).

rang*e* **;** *d, +ging, *r, * finder, ar*, de*, disar*, prear*, +k,
+ker, +kest, +kly, +kness, out+k, ‖ +kle, +kled, +kling.

sad ; *der, *dest, *ly, *ness, *den, *dened, *dening.

some ; *body, *how, *thing, *time, *times, *where, tire*.

tend ; *ed, *ing, *er, at*, at*ance, *ency, *encies, *ered,
*ering, *on, +se, +sile, +sion, +sity, in+sity, +t,
+ted, +ting, +ter, +tmaker, con*, in*, superin*.

LESSON LIX.

trace ; *d, +ing, *r, *able, *ry, +table, (ı tabil′ity), +tile,
(+til′ity), +tion, con+tion, +tive, de+tive, at+tive).

ap per *tain*′ **;** *ing, (+ur′tenance, +ur′tenances, +ur′tenant).

clap ; *ped, *ping, *per, *board, *trap, thunder*.

class ; *ed, *ing, *mate, *ic, *ify, out*, * meeting, first-*.

com pel′ **;** *led, *ling, *lable, +ulsive, +ulsiveness, +ulsion.

com pete′ **;** *d, +ing, +itive, +itor, +itors, (+i′tion),
(+ent, +ently, +ence, in+ent, in+ence).

eu′lo gy **;** +ies, (+ium), +ize, +ized, +izing, +ist, (+is′tic).

ex clu*de'*; *d, +ding, +sion, +sive, +sively, +siveness.
ex pend'; *ed, *ing, *iture, +se, +siveness, in+sive.
fat*e*; *d, *ful, +al, +ally, +alism, +alist, (+al'ity).
fer'v*ent*; *ly, +ency, +id, +idly, +or.
gid'dy; +ier, +iest, +ily, +iness, *-headed.
in i'tia*l*; *s, +te, +ted, +ting, +tive, (+tion), +tory, un+ted.
in oc'u la*te*; *d, +ting, +tor, (+tion), +ble.
in sin'u at*e*; *d, +ing, +ive, +or, +ingly, (+ion).
in her'it; *ed, *ing, *ance, *or, *ress, dis*ed, +age.
joy; *ful, *fully, *fulness, *ous, *ously, over*ed.
mag'ne*t*; *ize, *ized, *ism, *ic, (*o-electric'ity), ‖ (+sia).

LESSON LX.

no; *where, *thing, *wise, *t, *ne, (*nen'tity),*nesuch.
nom'*i nal*; *ly, +inate, (+inee'), (+ina'tion, +encla'ture).
per sist'; *ed, *ing, *ingly, *ent, *ently, *ence, *ency.
per'son; *ally, *ate, (*al'ity, *al'ities, *a'tion), (*ify), im*al.
pock'et; *ed, *ing, *book, *knife, * piece, pick*.
re mi*t*; *ted, *ting, un*ting, *tance, *tal, *tent, +ss' +ss'ness.
sec'*tion*; *al, *alism, dis+, dis+ed, dis*, bi+, bi*.
sus pend'; *ed, *ing, *er, +se, +sion, +se account.
sweat; *y, *iness, *er, *ed, *ing, * box.
sym'pa thy; +ies, +ize, +ized, +izing, (un+et'ic).
wel*l*; +fare, *-informed, *-known, *wisher, *-read, *-favored,
   *-bred, *-born, *doer, ‖ *s, *drain, * sinker.
art; *ful, *fully, *ifice, *isan, *ist, *lessness, (*ifi'cial).
brav*e*; *r, *st, *ly, *ry, +o, (+a'do, +a'does).
bur'den; *ed, *ing, *some, *someness, dis*, un*, over*.
con sum*e'*; *d, +ing, *r, +ptive, +ption, in+able.
con'ta*rt*;(+a'gious, +a'gion, +ig'uous, +in'gent, +in'gence).
con'tem plat*e*; *d, +ing, (+ive, +iveness), (+ion).
con tem*n'*; *ed, *ing, +pt, +pt'ible, +pt'uous, +pt'uously
con test'; *ed, *ing, *able, in*able, *ant, *anta

LESSON LXI.

dic'ta*te*; +ion, +ionary, +ating,(+a'tion, +a'tor),(+ato'rial).

di gest'; *ed, *ing, *ion, *ible, in*ible, un*ed.

flat; *ter, *test, *ness, *ten, *wise, *iron, *-headed, *s.

ful'gen*t*; *ly, +cy, ef*, ef*ly, ef+ce, ef+cy, re*, re+ce.

fund; *ed, *ing, *able, (*amen'tal), *s, sinking *, re*.

gir*d*; *er, *le, *ler, +t, +th, be*, be*ing, un*, un*ing.

hes'i ta*te*; *d, +ncy, +ting, un+ting, un+tingly, (+tion).

id'l o*m*; *s, (*at'ic, +syn'crasy), +t, (+tic), +cy.

in cise'; *d, +ing, +or, +ion, +ions, +ive.

math e mat'ic; *s, *ally, (*ian, *ians).

mil*e*; *age, *stone, statute *, +l, +lion, +lionaire.

min'is ter; *ed, *ing, (*ial, *ially), +y, (+a'tion, ad+a'tion).

nec'es *sary*; +aries, (+ity, +itous, +itate), un*.

no'b*le*; *r, *st, *ness, *man, +ly, (+il'ity), ig*.

o'pen; *ed, *ing, *er, *ly, *ness, *-handed, *-hearted, un*ed.

pro fi'cien*t*; *ly, +ce, +cy, un+cy, un*, un*ly.

prop'er; *ly, im*ly, *ty, (+i'ety, +i'etary, +i'etor, +i'etress).

rad'i *cal*; *ly, *ism, * sign, +icate, e+icate, +ish.

rea'son; *ed, *ing, *er, *s, *able, un*ableness.

sol*e*; *ly, +o, +oist, +itary, +itaire. +itude, (+il'oquy).

LESSON LXII.

sum; *med, *ming, *mary, *marily, *marize, (con*ma'tion).

vi'*tal*; *s, *ly, *ize, (*ity), * force, +gor, +gorous.

a cad'e m*y*; +ies, +ist, (+ic, +ical, +icals), (+i'cian).

a chiev*e*'; *d, +ing, *r, +able, *ment, un*d.

bi og'ra ph*y*; +ies, +er, auto*, (+ic, +ical).

con ceal'; *ed, *ing, *er, *able, *ment, un*ed.

con cei*ve*'; *d, +iving, +ivable, in+ivable, +ption, +it, +ited.

con tai*n*'; *ed, *ing, *able, +entment, (+inent).

dr*op*; *ped, *ping, *light, * letter, +ip, +ibble, rain*.

ef fect**'**; *ed,*ing,*ually,*ive, (+ ica'cious), + i'cient, + i'ciency.

ef fuse'; + ive, + ively, + iveness, + ion, + ions.

house; *d, + ing, *hold, *keeper, * dog, ware*, court*, out*.

i den'tic al; *ly, + fy, + fying, + fied, (+ fica'tion), + ty, + ties.

jour'ney; *ed, *ing, *man, + al, + alist, + alize, + alizing.

la ment'; *ed, *ing, un*ed, (*able, *ably), (*a'tion).

nov'el; *ty, *ist, (*ette'), + ice, (+ i'tiate).

old; *er, *est, *ness, *-fashioned, * style, * maid, *-womanish.

per ceive'; *d, un*d, + iving, + ptible, im + ptible, + ption.

per'fect; *ly, *ed, *ing, (*ion), im*, im*ly, (im*ion).

point; *ing,*er,*less, + oign'ant, + ungent, + unctual, + unctuate.

LESSON LXIII.

por tray'; *ed, *ing, *er, *al, (+ it, + iture).

po si'tion; im*, dis*, indis*, (+ ture, im + ture, + itive), dis + e.

sen'ate; + ator, (+ ato'rial), * chamber, + ile, (+ il'ity), + ior.

as cend'; *ed, *ing, *ency, + sion, *able, (+ t, + ts).

cen'ter; + al, + alize, (+ ic'ity, ec + ic'ity, + if'ugal, + ip'etal).

court; *ship, *house, *-martial, *-plaster, *eous, dis*eous,*esy.

cure; + able, in + able, + ative, + ate, + ious, + io, (+ ios'ity).

curt; *ly, *ness, (*ail', *ail'ed, *ail'ing, *ail'ment).

cus'tom; *ary, *er, *house, ac*, ac*ed, ac*ary.

due; *bill, + ty, + tiable, + teous, + tiful, un + tiful, + ly, un + ly.

em bar'rass; *ed, *ing, *ment, un*ed, dis*ment.

flesh; *ly, *y, *ier, *iest, *iness, * tint, proud *.

in di vid'u al; *ize, *ized, *s, *ism, (*ity).

ma'son; *s, *ry, (*ic), * wasp, stone *, Free*.

mock; *ed, *ing, *er, *ery, *ing bird, * sun, * orange.

plen'ty; + teous, + tiful, + tifully, (+ ipoten'tiary).

plumb; *ed, *ing, * line, *er, + met, + met line.

pow'der; *ed, *ing, *y, *mill, * puff, gun*, baking *.

au'di ble; + ibly, + ience, + it, + itor, + iphone, (+ ito'rium).

cap; *ped, *ping, *per, * paper, *e, *es, (*ar'ison).

LESSON LXIV.

cor rect'; *ed, *ing, *ness, *ly, *ive, in*, (+ igible, in + igible).
coun'cil; *man, *or, city *, || + sel, + seled, + seling, + selor.
count; *ed, *ing, *er, *ingroom, ac*, ac*ant, re*, re*ed,
    || *ess, *y, *y town, *y court, *y commissioners.
dem'on strate; *d, + ing, + or, (+ ive, + iveness), (+ ion).
e con'o my; + ize, + ized, + izing, + ist, (+ ic, + ical, + ically).
e ject'; *ed, *ing, *or, *ion, *ment, + ac'ulate, (+ acula'tion).
foot; *ed, *ing, *boy, *fall, *light, *note, *-sore, square *.
flu'ent; *ly, + ency, + id, (+ id'ity), + id ounce, electric + id,
    (af'*, af'*ly, af' + ence, con'*, con' + ence), (+ ctua'tion).
im peach'; *ed, *ing, *ment, *able, un*able, un*ably.
im pede'; *d, + ing, + itive, + iment, un*d, un + ing.
loose; *d, + ing, *ly, *n, *ned, *ning, *ness, un*d.
love; *d, + ing, *r, + able, *ly, *liness, *lier, *-sick, un*ly.
me'di ate; + ating, + ator, (+ a'tion), (+ ato'rial), inter*.
med'i tate; *d, + ing, + ive, (+ ion, + ions), pre*d, pre + ing.
milk; *ed, *ing, *er, *y, *iness, *maid, *man, + ch cow.
o'ral; *ly, + ator, (+ ator'ical, + ato'rio), (+ a'tion), + otund.
pane; window *, + el, + eled, + eling, im + el, im + eled.
prof'it; *ed, *ing, *able, *ably, *less, un*able, un*ably.

LESSON LXV.

pru'dent; *ly, + ce, (*ial, *ially), im*, im + ce, im*ly.
rear; *ed, *ing, || *ward, *most, * line, * admiral, * guard.
sol'id; *ly, (*ity, *ify, *ified), (ifica'tion), con*ate.
so lic'it; *ed, *ing, *or, *ous, *ude, (*a'tion), un*ed.
time; + ing, *r, *ly, un*ly, *keeper, *-honored, *-table, * ball.
ap pear'; *ing, *ance, *ed, + ent, + ently, (+ i'tion), dis*.
as so'ci ate; *d, + ing, + ive, (+ ion), dis*, dis*d, dis + ing.
chalk; *y, *iness, *cutter, * line, white *, red *, French *.
char'ac ter; (*is'tic, *is'tically), *ize, *ized, *izing, (*iza'tion).

di plo'ma; *cy, *tist, (*t), (*t'ic, *t'ically), ‖ *a.

di rect'; *ed, *ing, *er, *or, *ly, *ness, *ion, *ory, mis*, (in*).

face; *d, +ing, +ial, de*, (*tious, *tiously, *tiousness).

fig'ure; +ing, *r, *s, +ative, *head, dis*, dis*d, (con+a'tion).

high; *ly, *ness, *er, *est, *way, *wayman, *born, *-bred,
     *-church, *-handed, *-minded, *-strung, * tide, * school.

let'ter; *ed, *ing, *er, *press, * box, * carrier, drop *.

mail; *ed, *ing, *able, * bag, * train, * boat.

pulse; +ate, +ated, +ating, (+a'tion), im*, im+ive.

quench; *ed, *ing, *able, *less, *lessness, un*ed, un*able.

re ly'; +ied, *ing, +iable, +iance, un+iable, (+iabil'ity).

LESSON LXVI.

roof; *ed, *ing, *less, *s, un*, un*ed, un*ing, flat *.

room; *ed, *ing, *mate, *y, *ier, *iness, *ful, bed*, work*.

screw; *ed, *ing, un*, *-driver, * wrench, twin-* steamer.

touch; *ing, un*ed, *back, *down, *stone, *-paper, *-me-not.

two; *fold, *-edged, +ilight, +ill, +ice, +ain, +in, +elve.

type; *setter, *writer, +ify, +ical, (+og'raphy), daguerre'o*

add; *ed, *ing, *ible, (*ibil'ity), (*i'tion, *i'tional).

cau'tion; *ing, *er, *ary, +us, +usly, in+usly, in+usness.

con'science; *less, (+en'tious, +en'tiously), +ous, un+ously.

corn; *crib, *cob, *cutter, *field, *dodger, * cake, pop *, broom *.

coun'try; *man, *woman, * seat, +ify, +ified, +ies.

cour'age; (*ous, *ously), en*, en*d, en+ing, dis*, dis+ing.

cu'mu late; +ive, (+ion), ac*, ac+ing, ac+or. (ac+ion).

dream; *ed, *ing, *er, *y, *ier, *iest, *less, *lsnd. *s.

balm; *y, *ily, em*, em*ed, em*ing, em*er.

hu'mor; *ed, *ing, *ous, *ously, *some, *ist, good-*ed.

in spire'; *d, +ing, +able, +atory, (+a'tion), (+ator).

list; *ed, *ing, price *, en*, en*ed, en*ing. ‖ *less, *en.

lit'er a ry; +ature, +al, +ally, (+a'tim, al+a'tion), il+ate.

luck; *y, *ily, *less, *lessness, un*y, un*ily, *ier, *iest.

LESSON LXVII.

mine; *d, +ing, *r, +eral, +eralize, +eralist, (+eral'ogy).

mob; *bed, *bing, *s, *ile, *ilize, (im*il'ity), (*iliza'tion).

mode; +ish, (+iste'), +el, +eled, +eling, +ulate, +ulating, (ula'tion), +erate, +erately, (+era'tion), +ern, +ernness), +ernize, +est, +estly, +esty, +ify, +ified, (+ifica'tion).

plead; *ed, *er, inter*, im*, im*ed, im*er, +se, +sing, +sant, un+santness, +santry, +surable, +sure.

pon'der; *ed, *ing, *er, *able, im*able, *ous, *ously, *ousness.

pot; *ted, *ting, *s, (*a'tion), *ion, *ash, *pie, *ter, *ter's field.

roll; *ed, *ing, *er, *ing-pin, * call, *ing mill, un*.

ru'ral; *ist, +s'tic, +s'ticate, (+stic'ity), (+stica'tion).

ag gress'; *ed, *ing, *or, *ion, *ions, *ive, *ively, *iveness.

a maze'; *d, +ing, +ingly, *ment, un*d.

blas pheme'; *d, +ing, *r, (+ous, +ously, +y, +ies).

change; +ing, *able, *ableness, *less, ex*, ex*able, inter*able.

chirp; *ed, *ing, +rup, +ruped, +ruping, +rupy.

con grat'u late; *d, +ing, +or, +ory, (+ion).

con trol'; *led, *ling, *ler, *lable, *ment, un*lable.

de nounce'; *d, *ment, +iator, +iate, +iative, (+ia'tion).

de stroy'; *er, +uc'tive, +uc'tively, +uc'tiveness, +uc'tion.

LESSON LXVIII.

de spair'; *ingly, (+era'do, +era'tion), (+erate, +erately).

for'tune; +nate, +nately, * teller, mis*, un+nate, (+itous).

frac'tion; *al, in*, +ctious, +cture, +gile, (+gil'ity), +gment.

God; *ly, *liness, *father, *send, *speed, *-fearing, +od-bye.

in flame'; *d, +ing, +mable, +matory, (+ma'tion).

pen'al; *ty, +itent, im+itent, +itence, (+iten'tiary).

pen'sion; *ed, *ing, *er, *s, +ve, +vely, +veness.

rem'e dy; +ies, +ied, *ing, (+iable, +ial, +ially).

sci'ence; (+tif'ic, +tif'ically), (con*), (con+tious).

spri*ng*; +ung, *ing, *y, *ier, *iest, * mattress, * wagon, *s,
 *let, *head, +inkle, +inkled, +inkling, +inkler, ‖ *time.
fac*t*; *ion,*ious,*iously,*iousness,(*i'tious),*or,*ory,+sim'ile.
fai*l*; *ing, un*ing, *ure, +lacy, (+la'cious), +lible, in+lible.
hab'i*t*; *s, (*uate, *ual, *ually), in*, in*ed, in*ant.
heav*e*; +ing, +er, up*, +y, +ier, +iest, +ily, +iness, top+y.
lib'er *al*; *ly, (*ity, il*ity), +ate, +ated, +ating, +ty, +ties.
cal'um n*y*; +ies, (+iate, +iated, +iating, +iator).
de bauch'; *ed, *ing, *ery, *ment, (*ee'), un*ed.
mall; *ed, *ing, *eable, im*eable, (*eabil'ity, im*eabil'ity).
nar rat*e'*; *d, +ing, +or, +ion, (+ive).

LESSON LXIX.

palm; *ed, *ing, *istry, ‖ (*et'to), * oil, * wine, ✳ Sunday.
tain*t*; *ed, *ing, un*ed, at*, at*ment, bill of at+der.
Amer'i ca; *n, *nize, *nized, *nizing, *nism, Pan-✳n.
broad; *er, *est, *ly, *cast, *side, *-brimmed, * gauge, a*.
choi*ce*; *r, *st, *ly, *ness, +ose, +osing, +se, +sen.
form; *ed, *ing, *al, *ally, *ulate, *ula, re*, uni*, in*, unin*ed.
ge'ni a*l*; *ly, (*ity), un*, con*, con*ly, (con*ity), uncon*.
hen; *bane, *coop, *nery, *pecked, *roost, turkey *.
hor'*ror*; +ible, +ibly, +id, +idly, +ify, +ified, *-struck.
in cline'; *d, +ing, +able, (+a'tion), dis*d, (dis+a'tion).
in'flu en*ce*; *d, +cing, (+tial), (+za), un*d, un+cing.
le*nd*; *er, *ing, +oan, +oaned, +oaning, +oans, +oan office.
mad; *der, *dest, *ly, *ness, *house, *den.
plat*e*; *d, +ing, *r, *ful, +ter, +eau, +form, +itude, *glass.
pound; *ed, *ing, *age, *cake, *-rate, *keeper, im*, im*ed.
re'g*al*; *ly, (*ia), +ent, +ency, +icide, +imen, +iment,
 +ular, +ularly, (+ular'ity), +ulate, +ulating, (+ula'tion).
wish; *ed, *ing, *es, *ful, *fully, *fulness, *bone.
coat; *ed, *ing, *less, (waist*ing), *s, over*, dress *.
de cid*e'*; *d, +ding, +sive, +sively, +siveness, +sion, un*d.

LESSON LXX.

lav*e*; +v′atory, +undry, +v′ender, +va, +vish, +vishly.

ma*k*e; +de, *r, *weight, *shift, *-up, *-believe.

nour′*ish*; *ed, *ing, *ment, +rse, +triment, (+tri′tious).

qui′e*t*; *ed, *ing, *ly, *ude, (*tus), dis*, dis*ude, (ac+sce′).

rat′tl*e*; *d, +ing, *r, *box, *snake, *s.

beau′ty; +ies, +eous, +iful, +ifully, +ify, +ified, +ifier.

mark; *ed, *ing, *er, *sman, *s, trade-*, pock*.

neu′te*r*; +al, (+al′ity), +alize, +alizer, (+aliza′tion).

part; *ly, *ial, *ially, (im*ial′ity), *isan, *ner, *i-colored,
(*ake, *aken, *aking, *aker, *ic′ipate, *ic′ipant, *ic′ularize).

re sist′; *ed, *ing, *ance, *ant, *less, *ible, ir*ible, ir*ibly.

sol′emn; *ly, *ness, (*ity), *ize, *ized, *izing.

spel*l*; +t, *ing, *er, *ing book, *ing bee, ‖ *s, *bound.

splen′d*or*; *s, +id, +idly, re+ent, re+ently, re+ence.

stead; *fast, *fastness, *y, *ier, *iest, *iness, un*y, in*, bed*.

stiff; *en, *ening, *ly, *ness, *er, *est, *-necked.

stop; *ped, *ping, *per, un*ped, * watch, *-over ticket, short*.

su′gar; *ed, *y, *house, *plum, * bowl, * candy, maple *.

sun; *rise, *set, *ny, *nier, *niest, *burn, *bonnet, *light,
*ned, *ning, *-dried, *flower, *glass, * stroke, *-struck, ✷day.

LESSON LXXI.

wid*e*; *ly, *ness, *r, *st, *spread, +en, *-awake, world-*.

won′de*r*; *ed, *ing, *ful, *fully, +ous, +ously, *-worker

an′a ly*ze*; *d, +zing, *r, +st, (+sis, +ses), (+t′ically).

an nul′; *led, *ling, *lable, *ment, dis*, dis*led.

de mur′; *s, *red, *ring, *rer, *rage, *rable.

germ; *inate, (*ina′tion), *inal, disease *, (*ane′).

gre ga′ri *ous*; *ly, *ness, (ag+ted, ag+ting), ag+tion.

gri*e*f; +ve, +ving, +vous, +vously, +vousness, +vance.

hum′*ble*; *d, +bling, +bly, (+il′iate, +il′ity), (+ilia′tion).

in'di cate; *d, +ing, +or, *s, (+ion), (+ive).
in fer'; *red, *ring, *able, (*ence), (*en'tial, *en'tially).
lux'u ry; +ies, (+ious, +iously, +iance, +iant, +iantly).
north; *east, *west, *ern, *erner,+seman,+way,(+we'gian).
ap pre hend'; *ing, +sion, +sive, mis*, mis*ed, mis+sion.
ap prove'; +ving, +vingly, +val, (+ba'tion), dis*, dis+val.
ar'bi ter; +ate, +ated, +ary, +arily, (+ament), (+a'tion).
boun'ty; +ies, +iful, +ifully, +eous, +eously, * jumper.
can'vas; *back, * tent, ‖ *s, *sed, *sing, *ser.
cite; re*, re+al, (+a'tion, re+ative', re+a'tion), in*.
con ve'ni ent; *ly, +ce, in*, in*ly, in+ce, in+cing.

LESSON LXXII.

dex'ter; *ous, *ously, (*ity), ambi+ous, ambi+ously.
en'gine; *s, (+eer', +eer'ing, civil +eer'), fire *.
found; *ing, *er, *ress, (*a'tion), un*ed, ‖ *ry, *ries, ‖ +t.
friend; *ly, *liness, *less, *ship, un*ly, un*liness, *s, be*ed.
pre sent'; *ed, *ing, *able, *ment, (*a'tion), (*s), un*able.
press; *ing, *er, *es, *ure, *man, im*, re*, irre+ible, com*ed.
ar'bor; *s, *ed, *ist, (*es'cent), (*icul'ture), * vine, * day.
cease; *s, *d, in+sant, in+santly, in+sancy, (+sa'tion).
com plete'; *ly,*ness,*r,*st,+tion,(+ment),(+men'tary),in*.
com pre hend'; *ed, *ing, +sive, +sion, +sible, in+sible.
con vene'; +ient, in+ient, +ience, in+ience, (+t), +tion.
dai'ry; +ies, *ing, *maid, *man, *woman, * farm.
de sign'; *ed, *ing, *er, *edly, *able, (*ate, *ated), (*a'tion).
dress; *er, *y, *maker, *ing room, * goods, un*, top-*ing.
print; *ed, *ing, *s, *er, *ing ink, *ing office, im*, mis*.
con serve'; *d, +ing, +ative, +atively, +atism,+atory, (*s).
con spire'; *d, +ing, +acy, +acies, +ator.
co quet'; *ted, *ting, *ry, *tish, *tishly, *tishness, *te, *tes.
cor res pond'; *ed, *ing, *ingly, *ent, *ents, *ence.
creed; *s, +ence, +ible, in+ible, +it, (+en'tial, +u'lity).

LESSON LXXIII.

da*y*; +ily, *book, *break, *light, *-laborer, * school, Mon*.
dr*y*; +ier, +iest, +ied, sun-+ied, *ly, *ness, *-rub, * goods.
mud; *dy, *diness, *dier, *diest, *dle, *dled, *hole, * scow.
mys'te *ry*; +eries, (+e'rious), +ic, +ical, +icism, (+ify'ing).
pur*e*; *r, *st, *ly, +ity, +itan, +ge, +gative, +ify, im*.
pur su*e'*; *d, +ing, *r, +it, +able, +ance, +ant.
pu*s*; +trid, (+trid'ity), +trefy, +trefied, (+tres'cence).
rock; *y, *iness, *fish, * candy, ‖ *er, *away, *ing-horse, ‖ *et.
re serv*e'*; +ing, +edly, +edness, +atory, *s, (+a'tion), (+oir).
re sid*e'*; *r, (+ence, +ent, non+ent, +ue), +ual, +uary.
re stor*e'*; *d, +ing, *r, +able, +ative, +atives, (+a'tion).
re solv*e'*; +ving, +vent, un+vable, (+ute, +utely), (+u'tion).
re tal'i at*e*; *d, +ing, +ive, +ory, (+ion).
sen*se*; *less, (+sa'tion), (;sibil'ity), +sitive, +sual, +suous,
　　+tence, (ten'tious), +tient, +timent, (+timental'ity).
sep'a ra*te*; *d, +ting, *ly, +ble, in+ble, +tor, (+tion).
shell; *er, *y, *fish, *bark, *proof, *-less, * road, oyster *.
spea*k*; *er, *ership, +ech, +echless, +echlessness, un*able.
spe'*cies*; +ial, +ialist, +ialty, +ie, +ify, (+if'ic), (+ifica'tion),
　　+imen, +ious, +tacle, (+ta'tor), +ter, +ulate, (+ula'tion).

LESSON LXXIV.

steam; *ed, *ing, *er, *boat, *ship, * engine.
stock; *ed, *jobber, *holder, * account, * yard, *ing, *ade.
st*y*; +ile, +ep, +eps, +air, +airs, +aircase, +airway.
trem'*ble*; *d, +bling, +or, +ulous, (+en'dous, +en'dousness).
trib*e*; *s, +al, +une, (+u'nal), +ute, +utes, +utary, +utaries.
tru*e*; *ness, *-hearted, +th, un+thful, +st, (+stee'), mis+st.
vag*ue*; *ly, *ness, +rant, +rancy, +abond, +ary, +aries.
verb; *al, *iage, *ose, (*os'ity, *a'tim), *s, ad*, pro*.
vi'o la*te*; *d, +ating, +able, (+a'tion), +ator, +ence, +ent, in*.
viv'*id*; *ly, *ness, (+a'cious, +ac'ity), +ify, +ified, (+isec'tion).

void; *able, *ance, a*, a*ed, a*ing, a*able, una*able.

vo li'*tion*; +up'tuous, (+untary, in+untary), (+unteer').

con crete'; *ly, *ness, +ion, +ions, +ive, *d, +ing.

cord; *s, *age, *on, *uroy, *uroy road, *ed, *ing, * wood.

cor ro*de'*; +ding, +sive, +sively, +siveness, +sion, in+dible.

cross; *ed, *ing, *ly, *ness, *road, *-tie, *-eyed, *-examine, re*,
   +ucial, +uciate, ex+uciating, +ucify, +ucifix, +usade.

cre ate'; *d, +ing, +or, +ive, +iveness, + ion, (re+ion), +ure.

crime; *s, +inal, +inate, +inated, (+inal'ity, +ina'tion).

low; *er, *est, *ly, *ness, *er-case, *-pressure engine, be*.

COMMERCIAL TERMS.

LESSON LXXV.

ac cept'; *ed, *ing, *or, *able, *ance, *ances, (*a'tion).

ac count'; *ing, *ant, *s, * book, * current, * sales.

ac crue'; *d, +ing, *s.

ac cu'mu la*te*; *d, +ing, +ive, (+ion).

ac knowl'edg*e*; *d, +ing, *ment, *ments.

ad min'is ter; *ed, *ing, (+a'tor, +a'trix, +a'tion).

ad ver tis*e'*; *d, +ing, +er, (*ment).

ap prais*e'*; *d, +ing, +er, *ment.

ar'bi tra*te*; *d, +ing, +or, (+ion).

as sess'; *ed, *ing, *or, *able, *ment, *ments.

as sign'; *ed, *ing, *able, *s, (*ee', *or'), *ment.

as so'ci a*te*; *d, +ing, *s, (+ion), * member.

at tach'; *ed, *ing, (*e'), *able, *ment.

au'di*t*; *ed, *ing, *or, *ors, +ence, (*o'rium).

bal'anc*e*; *s, +ing, *d, * sheet, un*d, trial *, cash *.

bank; *ed, *ing, *er, * bill, * book, * note, * credit,
   * of deposit, * of issue, *rupt, *ruptcy, *rupt law.

bar'gain; *ed, *ing, *er, (*ee', *or'), *s.

bill; * book, *head, * receivable, * payable, way*, due*.

bond; *ing, *holder, *s, *sman, *ed goods, *ed warehouse.

LESSON LXXVI.

bus'y; +ier, +iest, +ily, +inesslike, +iness college.
cap'i tal; *ize, *ized, *ist, (*iza'tion), * stock.
cash; *ed, *ing, *ier, *book, * account, * boy, * sales.
cer'ti fy; +ied, *ing, +ier, +ied check, (+icate), (+ica'tion).
charge; *d, +ing, +er, *able, *s, dis*, over*.
char'ter; *ed, *ing, *s, * land, * member.
chat'tel; *s, * mortgage, personal *, real *.
check; *ed, *ing, *s, * book, * list, bank *.
clear; *ed, +ify, *ance, *ances, *ing house.
clerk; *ship, *s, +ical, entry *, shipping *, town *.
coin; *ed, *ing, *age, *s, * balance.
col lat'er al; *s, * assurance, * issue, * security.
col lect'; *ed, *ing, *ible, *or, *ion.
com bine'; *d, +ing, (+a'tion).
com'merce; (+ial law, +ial paper, +ial note paper)
com mis'sion; *ed, *ing, *s, *er, * merchant.
com'pa ny; +ies, insurance *, stock *, joint-stock *.
com'pen sate; *d, +ing, +ive, +or, (+ion).
com pete'; +itor, (+ence, +ency, +ent, in+ent), (+i'tion).
cor'po rate; (+ion aggregate, +ion sole), in*, * member.

LESSON LXXVII.

com'pro mise; *d, +ing, *r, *s.
com pute'; *d, +ing, +er, +able, (+a'tion).
con sign'; *ed, *ing, (*ee'), *or, *ment, *ments.
copy; +ied, +ier, *graph, *right, *ing ink, *ing press.
count; *er, *inghouse, dis*, ‖ ermand, *ermark, *ersign.
cred'it; *ed, *ing, *or, *s, (* foncier, * mobilier), bank *,
    *able, *ably, +ible, in+ible, +ulous, (+en'tial).
cur'ren cy; +cies, +t money, account +t.
cus'tom; *er, *ers, *s, *house, *house broker.

dam'ag*e*; *d, +ing, *able, *s, nominal *s, vindictive *a.
dat*e*; *d, +ing, *r, *s, *less, due *.
deal; *t, *ing, *ings, *er, retail *er, wholesale *er.
deb*t*; *or, *s, in*ed, +it, +ited, +iting.
deed; *ed, *ing, *s, quit-claim *, mortgage *.
de fau*lt'*; *ed, *ing, *er, (+cator), (+ca'tion).
de fea'*sance*; *d, +ible, +ibleness, in+ible, (in+ibil'ity).
de fl'*cient*; *ly, +ency, +encies, (+t).
de fray'; *ed, *ing, *er, *al, *ment.
de pos'it; *ed, *ing, *or, *ary, *s, *ory, (*ion).
de pre'ci at*e*; *d, +ing, +ive, +or, +ory, un*d.

LESSON LXXVIII.

dis burs*e'*; *d, +ing, *r, *ment, +ing officer.
dis crep'an*t*; +ce, +cy, +cies.
di vi*de'*; *d, +ding, +sion, (+dend).
dow'*er*; *ed, *less, +ry, +ager, en+, en+ment.
draft; *ed, *ing, *er, *s, sight *, time *.
draw; *n, *ing, *er, (*ee'), with*, with*al.
em bez'zl*e*; *d, +ing, *r, *ment.
em ploy'; *ed, *ing, *er, (*ee'), *ment, un*ed.
en gross'; *ed, *ing, *er, *ment, *ed bill, *ing hand.
eq'ui *ty*; +table, +value, (+v'alent, +v'ocate), (+voca'tion).
ex chang*e'*; *d, +ing, *s, * broker, telephone *.
ex'e cute; *d, +ing, (+ion), (+or, +rix, +ive).
ex pen*se'*; *s, +sive, +d, +ded, +ding, +diture, * account.
ex port'; *ed, *ing, *er, *able, (*a'tion), (*s).
fac'tor; *s, *age, *y, *ies, home *, foreign *, cotton *y.
fee; *d, *ing, *s, * simple, clerk's *s.
fl nanc*e'*; *s, +ial, +ially, (*ier'),
fix; *ed, *ing, gas *ture, store *tures.
fluc'tu at*e*; *d, +ing, (+ion).
for'eign; *er, * bill, * office, * exchange.

LESSON LXXIX.

for'feit; *ed, *ing, *able, *s, *er, *ure.
forg*e*; *d, +ing, *r, +ery, +eries.
for'ward; *ed, *ing, *er, *s, *ness.
fraud; *s, *ulence, *ulent, *ulently, de*, de*ed.
free; *d, *ing, *hold, * goods, * port, * trade.
freight; *ed, *ing, *er, *age, *s, * agent, * car, * train.
gain; *ed, *ing, *er, *s, loss and *, re*, re*ed.
gaug*e*; *d, +ing, *r, *able, +ing rod.
grant; *ed, *ing, *or, (*ee'), *able, *s.
guar an t*ee*'; *d, *ing, (+or, +y), written *, absolute *.
hon'*est*; *y, *ly, dis*, dis*y, +ored, +orary, dis+or.
im port'; *ed, *ing, *er, (*a'tion), *s.
in dem'ni *fy*; +fied, *ing, (+fica'tion), +ty, +ties.
in dors*e*'; *r, (*e'), blank *ment, full *ment, qualified *ment.
in fring*e*'; *d, +ing, *r, *ment.
in sol'ven*t*; +cy, * debtor, * law.
in stall'; *ed, *ing, (*a'tion), *ments, *ment house.
in vest'; *ed, *ing, *or, *ment, ‖ *igate, (*iga'tion).
in'voic*e*; *d, +ing, *s, outward *, inward *.
job; *bed, *bing, *ber, *s, * printer, * lot.

LESSON LXXX.

joint; *ly, *ure, * committee, * note, * bond, * tenant.
judg*e*; *d, +ing, *s, +ment, +ments, arrest of +ment.
law; *s, *yer, *ful, * book, common *, statute *, commercial *.
leas*e*; *d, +ing, *s, *hold, *holder, re*, re*d, re*ment.
le'gal; *ly, (*ity), *ize, *ized, il*, * cap, * tender, * claim.
let'ter; *press, * book, * box, * carrier, * paper, drop *,
    dead-* office, * of credit, * of license, *s patent.
li'a b*le*; (+il'ity, +il'ities, limited +il'ity), re*, unre*.
li'cens*e*; *d, +ing, *r, (*e'), *s, *d traffic.

4

liq'ui date; *d, +ing, (+ion), *d damages.

ma ture'; *d, +ing, +ity, date of +ity, im*.

mer'chant; *able, * ship, +chandise, +cantile agency.

mon'ey; *s, +etary, +etize, *-making, * broker, * order.

mo nop'o ly; +ies, +ize, +ized, +ist.

mort'gage; *d, +ing, +or, (*e'), * deed, chattel *.

ne go'ti ate; *d, +ting, +tor, (+tion), +tory, +ble paper.

net; *ted, *ting, * capital, * profit, * income, * weight.

o'pen; *ed, *ing, * account, re*, un*.

op'er ate; *d, +ing, +or, co*, co*d, co+ing, (co+ion).

par; *ity, * value, * of exchange, at *, above *, below *.

LESSON LXXXI.

part'ner; *s, *ship, silent *, co*ship.

pass; *es, * book, * check, *port, *enger.

pat'ent; *ed, *ing, *s, *able, (*ee'), * right, * office.

pawn; *ed, *ing, *able, *broker, *er, (*ee'), * ticket.

pay; *ed, *ing, *able, *er, (*ee'), *ment, *master, * day, * roll.

pol'i cy; +ies, *holder, insurance *, interest *, open *.

prop'er ty; (+i'etor, +i'etress, +i'etary medicine).

pro tect'; *ed, *ing, *or, *ive, *ion, *ive tariff.

pro test'; *ed, *ing, *er, (*a'tion), (*s, notice of *).

pur'chase; *d, +ing, *r, +able, *s, * money.

quar'an tine; *d, (+ing), * flag, * officer.

qual'i fy; +ied, *ing, (+ica'tion), +ied endorsement.

quote; *d, +ing, +able, (+a'tion).

rat'i fy; +ied, *ing, +ier, (+ica'tion), un+ied.

re ceive'; *d, +ving, *r, +pt, +pted, +pting, *s, bills +vable.

re deem'; *ed, *ing, *er, *able, +ption, ir*able.

re fer'; *red, *ring, (*ence, *able), (*ee').

re mit'; *ted, *ting, *tal, *tance, *tances, +ssion.

re'source; *s, (*ful, *less), * and liability account.

re spon'si ble; +ly, (+il'ity, +il'ities), ir*.

LESSON LXXXII.

sal*e*; +able, *s, *sman, *smen, whole*, un+able, bill of *.

se cur*e'*; *d, +ing, +ity, +ities, *ment, in*.

seiz*e*; *d, +ing, +able, +ure, dis*, dis+ure.

ship; *ped, *ping, *per, *ment, *load, * chandler, steam*.

shr*ink*; +ank, +unk, *ing, *age, un+unk.

sol'*vent*; +vency, in*, in+vency, dis+ve, (dis+u'tion).

stat*e*; *d, +ing, *ment, ‖ *s *sman, ✳ rights, ✳'s evidence.

stat'ut*e*; *s, +ory, +able, * law, * of limitations.

stip'u lat*e*; *d, +ing, +or, (+ion).

stock; *ed, *ing, *s, *holder, *broker, * company, * exchange.

su*e*; *d, +ing, +its, civil +it, criminal +it, non+it.

sum; *med, *ming, *s, *mary, *marily, *marize.

sur*e*; *r, *st, *ly, *ty, *ties, in*, as*, as+ance, reas*.

swin'dl*e*; *d, +ing, *r, *s.

tar'iff; *s, * reform, revenue *, protective *.

tax; *ed, *ing, *able, *es, (*a'tion), *payer, * collector.

tel'e *graph*; *ic, * cable, electric *, +gram, +phone.

tell; *ing, *er, *ership, bank *er.

ton; *s, short *, long *, *nage, gross *nage, net *nage.

to'tal; *ly, *s, (*ity), * loss, * gain.

LESSON LXXXIII.

trad*e*; *d, +ing, *r, *s, *sman, *-mark, * price, * discount.

traf'fic; *ked, *king, *ker, *less.

trans act'; *ed, *ing, *or, *ion.

trib'ut*e*; *s, +ary, +aries, con*, con+or, con+ory,(con+ion)

us*e*; *d, +ing, +er, +ury, +urer, (+u'rious), dis*.

val'id; *ate, (*ity), in*, in*ate, (in*ity).

val'u*e*; *d, +ing, *s, (+a'tion), +able consideration.

ven'tur*e*; *d, +ing, *r, *s, +ous, ad*, bill of ad*.

void; *ed, *ing, *er, *able, *ness, *ance, a*, una*able.

vouch; *ed, *ing, *ers, *er, (*ee'), *safe.

ware; *house, *room, *s, hard*, glass*, tin*.

war'rant; *ed, *ing, *y, *or, (*ee'), *s, bench *, search *.

af fi da'vit	grace	pro ra'ta
as'sets	in den'ture	re bate'
aux il'ia ry	in teg'ri ty	re voke'
bo'nus	in junc'tion	sched'ule
bul'lion	in'stant	scheme
con'sul	in'ven to ry	set-off
con'tra	ma'ker	sum'mon
cou'pon	man'i fest	syn'di cate
em po'ri um	mar'gin	tare
fac sim'i le	no'ta ry	tes'ti mo ny
firm	plain'tiff	tick'ler

PROFESSIONS AND OCCUPATIONS.

accountant	bank teller	bottler
actor	barber	brakeman
actress	basket	brasier
addresser	bell boy	bricklayer
aeronaut	bell founder	broker
astrologer	bell hanger	brushmaker
auctioneer	biographer	bundle boy
auditor	bicycler	butcher
author	blacksmith	butler
agent	bookkeeper	cabinetmaker
appraiser	bookbinder	calker
artist	book folder	canmaker
assayer	booking clerk	canvasser
axman	bookmaker	capmaker
baker	bookseller	capper
banker	bootblack	carder

carpenter	currier	evangelist
carpet layer	cutler	examiner
carpet sewer	cutter	farmer
cartman	dairymaid	farm hand
cashier	dairyman	feeder
catcher	dealer	finisher
caterer	dentist	fireman
chambermaid	designer	fisherman
chandler	detective	florist
chemist	digger	forelady
chiromancer	director	foreman
chronologer	dishwasher	fruiterer
cigarmaker	distiller	furrier
clerk	ditcher	gardener
clergyman	diver	glass blower
cloakmaker	doctor	glazier
coachman	dramatist	glover
cobbler	draughtsman	gold beater
collarmaker	drayman	goldsmith
collector	dressmaker	governess
collier	driver	grainer
compositor	drover	grazier
conductor	drug clerk	gripman
confectioner	druggist	grocer
contractor	drummer	groom
conveyancer	dyer	gunner
cook	editor	gunsmith
cooper	educator	hairdresser
coppersmith	electrician	hall man
cornetist	elevator boy	harnessmaker
coroner	embroiderer	hatter
cowboy	engineer	hodman
crimper	engraver	horseshoer
crocheter	entry clerk	hosier

hotel man	marker	peddler
housecleaner	mason	perfumer
housekeeper	mechanic	photographer
huckster	mercer	physician
hydrographer	merchant	pianist
importer	messenger	pianomaker
inspector	metal spinner	piano tuner
instructor	miller	pilot
inventor	milliner	pitcher
iron founder	millwright	plasterer
janitor	miner	plumber
japanner	minister	policeman
jeweler	minstrel	polisher
jobber	moulder	politician
job printer	musician	porter
jockey	navigator	preacher
joiner	newsboy	presser
journalist	novelist	pressman
kitchenmaid	nurse	printer
laborer	oculist	prize fighter
laundress	office boy	professor
laundryman	oiler	proof reader
lawyer	operator	publisher
letter carrier	optician	reporter
lineman	organist	retoucher
linguist	organizer	roofer
lithographer	overseer	ropemaker
lumberman	oysterman	sailor
lunch man	packer	salesman
machinist	painter	sampler
magician	paper cutter	sawyer
manager	paper hanger	scraper
manufacturer	paver	seaman
mariner	pawnbroker	seamstress

secretary	stove dealer	upholsterer
sexton	surgeon	usher
shipping clerk	tailor	varnisher
shipwright	teacher	waiter
shoemaker	teamster	warden
slater	tentmaker	watchmaker
solderer	tinner	watchman
soldier	tinsmith	weaver
solicitor	tobacconist	weigher
stableboy	trainer	well sinker
stableman	transcriber	wharfinger
stenographer	tutor	wheelwright
stevedore	typewriter	wire-worker
stock jobber	umbrellamaker	wood chopper
stoker	undertaker	wood engraver
storekeeper	underwriter	wood turner

NAMES OF ARTICLES OF MERCHANDISE.

DRUGS.

ac'id	brim'stone
ac'o nite	bu'chu (bu'ku)
al'co hol	cam'phor (kam'fer)
al'oe (al'o)	can thar'i des (—i deez)
al'um	cas'sia (kash'a)
am mo'nia	cas'tor oil (kas'ter oil)
ar'ni ca	cham'o mile (kam'o mile)
ar'se nic	cin cho'na (sin ko'na)
as a fœt'i da (as a fet'i da)	chlo'ro form (klo'ro form)
bel la don'na	cod-liver oil
ben zine' (ben zeen')	cooh'i neal (kotch'i neel)
ben zoin'	cop'per as
bo'rax	cream of tar'tar (tar'ter)

cu'bebs
dye (di)
er'got
gam'bier (gam'beer)
gam boge' (gam booj')
gin'seng (jin'seng)
glyc'er in (glis'er in)
i'o dine (i'o din)
ip e cac u an'ha (—an'a)
jal'ap
lau'rel
lic'o rice (lik'o ris)
mad'der
man'na
mor'phi a (—fi a)

nut'gall
o'pi um
pot'ash
phos'phor us (fos'for us)
quick'sil ver
qui'nine (kwi'nine)
rhu'barb (ru'barb)
sar sa pa ril'la
seid'litz (sed'lits)
sen'e gal
sen'na
shel'lac
so'da
va nil'la
vit'ri ol (vit'ri ul)

DRY GOODS.

ar'mure
ar mo zeen'
al pac'a
As tra khan' (as tra kan')
ba rege' (ba raizh')
Bed'ford cord
Ben gal'(ben gawl') stripes
broad'cloth
bro cade' (bro kade')
bro'ca tel (bro'ka tel)
buck'ram
cal'i co
cam'bric (kaim'brik)
can'vas
cash'mere
cas'si mere (kas'si mer)
cas si nette' (kas si net')

cheese cloth
chev'i ot (shev'i ut)
Chi'na silk
cor'du roy
cot'ton ade
crash
crape
cre'pon
cre tonne' (kre ton')
cro chet' (kro shay')
dam'ask
de beige' (de baizh')
di ag'o nal cloth
doe'skin (do'skin)
dom'ett (dom'et)
dra'per y
edg'ing

em broi'der y

flan'nel

fich'u (fish'u)

gauze

gimp (ghimp)

ging'ham (ging'am)

gren a dine' (gren a deen')

Hen ri et'ta cloth

hick'o ry

Jac quards' (jak kards')

Jap a nese' silk

jean (jain)

lace

lin'en

lin'sey (lin'cy)

Mar seilles' (mar sailz')

me ri'no (me re'no)

mo'hair

mos qui'to (ke'to) netting

mus'lin (muz'lin)

or'gan die (or'gan dy)

or'gan zine (or'gan zin)

per cale' (per kal')

per ca line' (per ka leen')

pi que' (pe kay')

pol'ka-dot

pin-spot

pop'lin

plush

rib'bon

ruch'ing (roosh'ing)

sat'in

sat i net'

sheet'ing

Scotch plaid (plad)

scrim

seal plush

silk

si le'si a (sil le'shi a)

stock i net'

su'rah (soo'ra)

taf'fe ta

tape

tap'es try

tick'ing

tow'el ing

tram

trim'mings

twilled cotton

un'der wear

up hol'ster y

veil'ing (vail'ing)

ve lours' (ve loor')

vel'vet

vel vet een'

wad'ding

whip-cord

wrap

wig'an

yarn

---

bath robe

bal mor'al skirt

bead trimming

bi'as facing

blan'ket

blaz'er (blaiz'er)

blouse (blouz) waist

cloak

com'fort a ble

cor'set

coun'ter pane

hand'ker chief (—chif)

Jer'sey waist

muf'fler

pil'low case

pil'low sham

pin'a fore

por tiere' (por tyair')

quilt

reef'er

robe

scarfs

shawl

shirt

stock'ings

smok'ing jacket

ta'ble cover

trousseau' (troo so')

FLOWERS.

a lys'sum (a lis'sum)

a nem'o ne

ar'bu tus

a za'le a

be go'ni a

but'ter cup

car na'tion

chrys an'the mum

clem'a tis

cy'press

daf'fo dil

dah'lia (dal'ya)

dai'sy (da'zy)

dan'de li on (dan'de li un)

eg'lan tine (eg'lan tin)

fleur-de-lis (flur de le')

fuch'si a (fu'sha)

ge ra'ni um

he'li o trope

hol'ly hock

hy'a cinth (hi'a sinth)

hy dran'ge a (hy dran'je a)

ja pon'i ca

jas'mine (jas'min)

li'lac

lil'y

mar'i gold

mi gnon ette' (min yun et')

nar cis'sus

nas tur'tium(nas tur'shum)

or'chid (or'kid)

pan'sy (pan'zy)

pe'o ny

pe tu'ni a

phlox (floks)

rho do den'dron

rose

sun'flow er

sy rin'ga (syr in'ga)

tu'lip

ver be'na

vi'o let

FRUITS.

ap'ple

a'pri cot

ba na'na

black'ber ry

can'ta loupe (—loop)

cher'ry

cit'ron (sit'run)

date

dew'ber ry

fig

gage

goose'ber ry

grape

lem'on

mul'ber ry

ol'ive

or'ange

peach

pear

per sim'mon (—mun)

pine'ap ple

plum

pome'gran ate (pum—)

prune

quince

rai'sin (ra'z'n)

rasp'ber ry (raz'ber ry)

straw'ber ry

wa'ter mel on (—un)

whor'tle ber ry (hwurt—)

FURNITURE.

bed'stead (bed'sted)

black'board

brack'et

bric'-a-brac

buf fet' (boof fa')

bu'reau (bu'ro)

cab'i net

chair

chif fo nier' (shif fo neer')

count'er

cup'board (kub'berd)

desk

di van' (div van')

dumb'-wait er (dum—)

ea'sel (e'z'l)

fold'ing bed

ham'per

hat'rack

hall piece

lounge (lounj)

mir'ror (mir'rer)

ot'to man

ped'es tal

re frig'er a tor (—fridg—)

rock'ing-chair

rock'ing-horse

shelv'ing

side'board

show case

so'fa

stool

ta'ble

tow'el rack
tow'el ring
tete-a-tete' (tate-a-tate')

um brel'la stand
ward'robe
wash'stand

GEMS.

am'e thyst
ber'yl
car'bun cle
car nel'ian (car neel'yan)
chal ced'o ny (kal sed'o ny)
chrys'o lite (kris'o light)
crys'tal
di'a mond (di'mund)
em'er ald
gar'net

jas'per
o'nyx (o'niks)
o'pal
pearl (purl)
ru'by
sap'phire (saf'ire)
sar'di us
sar'do nyx (sar'do niks)
to'paz
tur quoise' (tur koiz')

GROCERIES AND PROVISIONS.

all'spice
ba'con
beans
buck'wheat
cakes
can'ned goods
cheese
choc'o late
cit'ron (sit'run)
cloves
cof'fee
con fec'tion e ry
corn meal
corned beef
crack'ers
e vap'o rated fruit
flour

gel'a tin
gin'ger
hom'i ny
hon'ey (hun'y)
in'di go
ker'o sene oil
lard
mace
mac a ro'ni
mo las'ses
mus'tard
nut'meg
ol'ive oil
peas
pep'per
pre serves'
rice

sal e ra'tus

salt

sug'ar (shoog'er)

syr'up (sir'up)

tap i o'ca

tea

ver mi cel'li (ver me sel'li)

vin'e gar

yeast (yeest)

yeast powder

HARDWARE.

an'vil

ax'le (ax'l)

bal'ance

bar iron

beam

bolt

brace

brack'et

brads

buck'le

cast'ers

chain

clamp

cleat

clew

clips

com'passes (kum').

cork'screw

cut'lery

damp'er (dam'per)

door bell

door spring

fau'cet

file

fork

gouge

hand'cuff

hoe

hol'der

hook

horse'shoe

husk'er

ket'tle

key

knife

knob

latch

lock

muz'zle

nails

oil'er

pad'lock

pul'ley

reg'is ter

riv'et

sash balance

si'phon (si'fon)

spike

steel'yard (stil'yurd)

type

valve

ven'ti la tor

wire

wrought iron

ARTISANS' TOOLS.

au'ger	jack'screw
ax	lev'el
adz	nail puller
awl	nip'pers
bill hook	pick'ax
bit	pin'cers
brace	plane
chis'el	punch
cleav'er	ring'er
draw'ing knife	saw
drill	screw-driver
hatch'et	shov'el
ham'mer	spade
ice pick	wrench

LUMBER.

beams	plank
boards	posts
cas'ing (ka'sing)	rims
ceil'ing	scant'ling
fel'loe (fel'lo)	shin'gles
fen'cing	ship-lap
fin'ish ing	shut'ters
floor'ing	sills
hubs	staves
joist	strips
laths	stud'ding
pales	wa'gon bot'toms

MACHINES AND IMPLEMENTS

bind'er	corn cutter
boil'er	corn'sheller
chain pump	cot'ton gin
corn planter	cul'ti va tor

der'rick
e lec'tric engine
fire en'gine
grain drill
har'row
hay press
hay-cutter
hay'rake
mow'er
plow
print'ing press

reap'er
roll'er
sew'ing machine
steam engine
stone crusher
straw-cutter
stump puller
ted'der
thresh'er
type'setter
type'writer

STATIONERY.

al'bums
books
cards
e ras'er (e race'er)
en'vel opes
games
ink
inkstands
pa'perweights

pen'holders
pen'rack
pen'cils
pens
rul'er
tab'lets
val'en tines
writ'ing desks
writing pa'per

VEGETABLES.

as par'a gus
beans
beet
cab'bage
car'rot (car'rut)
cau'li flow er (—flou er)
cel'e ry (sel'er y)
cu'cum ber
let'tuce (let'tis)
on'ion (un'yun)

pars'ley
pars'nip
po ta'to
pump'kin
rad'ish
sal'si fy
spin'ach (spin'age)
squash (skwosh)
to ma'to
tur'nip

VEHICLES.

am'bu lance

ba rouche' (ba roosh')

bi'cy cle (bi'sik'l)

ɔug'gy

ca'ble car

car'riage (kar'ridge)

cart

cou pe' (koo pay')

dray

e lec'tric car

freight car

han'som (han'sum)

hearse (hurse)

om'ni bus

pas'sen ger car

pha'e ton

sleep'ing car

sleigh (slay)

sur'rey (sur'ry)

sulk'y

tal'ly ho

tri'cy cle (tri'sik'l)

ve loc'i pede

vic to'ri a

wag'on (—un)

wheel'bar row (—bar ro)

WOODS.

al'der

ap'ple

ash

asp'en (as'pen)

beech

birch

box

but'ter nut

ca tal'pa

ce'dar (se'der)

cher'ry

chest'nut (ches'nut)

cy'press

dog'wood

eb'on y

elm

gum

hem'lock

hick'o ry

i'ronwood

i'vy

lo'cust

mag no'li a

ma hog'a ny

ma'ple

oak

pal met'to

per sim'mon

pine

pop'lar (—ler)

red'wood

rose'wood

sas'sa fras

syc'a more (sic—)

wal'nut (wol'nut)

wil'low (wil'lo)

COMMERCIAL ABBREVIATIONS AND SYMBOLS.

CAUTION.—Sentences, proper names, direct quotations or words used *very prominently*, should begin with capital letters. Most abbreviations form their plurals by adding *s*, and most symbols by adding *'s*.

above,	*abv.*	average,	*av.*
accent,	'	bag,	*bg.*
account,	%	balance,	*bal.*
account of Sales,	*Acct. Sales.*	bale,	*bl.*
add,	+	bank,	*bk.*
administrator,	*admr.*	banking,	*bank.*
admiral,	*Adml.*	barrel,	*brl.*
administratrix,	*admx.*	basket,	*bkt.*
adventure,	*adv.*	Bill Book,	*B. B.*
advertise,	*adv.*	bill of lading,	*b/l.*
advertisement,	*ad.*	bill payable,	*B. Pay.*
afternoon,	*P. M.*	bill receivable,	*B. Rec.*
agent,	*agt.*	bill of sale,	*b/s.*
all right,	*O. K.*	black,	*blk.*
alley,	*Al.*	bought,	*Bot.*
America,	*A.*	book,	*bk.*
amount,	*amt.*	box,	*bx.*
and so forth,	*&c.*	brought,	*brot.*
answer,	*ans.*	bushel,	*bu.*
April,	*Apr.*	by the year,	*per an.*
as above (*ut supra*),	*u. s.*	captain,	*Capt.*
assistant,	*asst.*	Cashbook,	*C. B.*
assorted,	*assd.*	cashier,	*Cash.*
at,	@	cent,	*ct.* or *ℓ.*
at pleasure (*ad libitum*),	*ad lib.*	charge,	*chg.*
attorney,	*atty.*	charged,	*chgd.*
August,	*Aug.*	cartage,	*ctge.*
avenue,	*Ave.*	Check Book,	*Ck. B.*

5

check,	*ck.*	dollar or dollars,	**$**
check mark,	✓	doctor of laws,	*LL.D.*
chest,	*ch.*	dozen,	*doz.*
Christmas,	*Xmas*	drayage,	*dray.*
civil engineer,	*C. E.*	each,	*ea.*
clerk,	*clk.*	east,	*E.*
collect on delivery,	*C. O. D.*	edition,	*ed.*
collection,	*coll.*	embroidered,	*embd.*
colonel,	*Col.*	entered,	*entd.*
colored,	*col'd*	entry,	*ent.*
commercial,	*coml.*	errors and omissions excepted,	
commission,	*com.*		*E. & O. E.*
commissioner,	*Com.*	errors excepted,	*E. E.*
commodore,	*Commo.*	esquire (title),	*Esq.*
company,	*Co.*	example,	*ex.*
consignment,	*con.*	exchange,	*exch.*
county,	*Co.*	executive committee,	*ex. com.*
court house,	*C. H.*	executor,	*exec.*
corner,	*cor.*	executrix,	*execx.*
corresponding secret'y,	*Cor. Sec.*	favor,	*fav.*
creditor,	*Cr.*	February,	*Feb.*
Daybook,	*D. B.*	figured,	*figd.*
days after date,	*d. d.*	firkin,	*fir.*
days after sight,	*d. s.*	first class,	*A. 1.*
deadhead,	*D. H.*	fixture,	*fixt.*
debtor,	*Dr.*	folio,	*fol.*
December,	*Dec.*	for example,	*e. g.*
department,	*dept.*	foreign,	*for.*
deposit,	*dep.*	forenoon,	*A. M.*
discount,	*dis.*	forward,	*ford.*
discounted,	*disctd.*	free on board	*F. O. B.*
district,	*Dist.*	freight,	*frt.*
doctor of medicine,	*Dr.* or *M.D.*	from,	*fr.*
doctor of divinity,	*D. D.*	Friday,	*Fri.*

furniture,	*fur.*	Ledger folio,	*L. F.*
gallon,	*gal.*	lieutenant,	*Lieut.*
general,	*Gen.*	madame (title),	*Mme.*
gentlemen (title),	*Messrs.*	manufacturer,	*mfr.*
grain,	*gr.*	manufacturing,	*mfg.*
great gross,	*g. gro.*	manuscript,	*MS.*
gross,	*gro.*	March,	*Mar.*
governor (title),	*Gov.*	mister (title),	*Mr.*
guaranty,	*guar*	Member of Congress,	*M. C.*
half,	*hf.*	memorandum,	*mem.*
handkerchief,	*hdkf.*	merchandise,	*mdse.*
hogshead,	*hhd.*	Mistress (title),	*Mrs.*
honorable (title),	*Hon.*	month,	*mo.*
hundred,	*C.* or *hund.*	multiplied by or by,	$\times$
hundredweight,	*cwt.*	namely,	*viz.*
inch or inches,	*in.*	National,	*Nat.*
instant,	*inst.*	new account,	*"/a.*
insurance,	*ins.*	next month,	*prox.*
interest,	*int.*	noon,	*M.*
inventory,	*invt.*	north,	*N.*
invoice,	*inv.*	notice or take notice,	*N. B.*
Invoice Book,	*I. B.*	October,	*Oct.*
January,	*Jan.*	o'clock,	*⁰/c.*
Journal,	*J.*	old account,	*⁰/a.*
Journal folio,	*J. F.*	one and one-fourth,	*1¹.*
junior,	*Jr.*	one and two-fourths,	*1².*
keg,	*kg.*	one and three-fourths,	*1³.*
last month.	*ult.*	on the passage,	*in trans.*
northeast,	*N. E.*	Order Book,	*O. B.*
northwest,	*N. W.*	ounce (avoirdupois or troy),	*oz.*
pound (avoirdupois),	*lb.*	ounce (apoth.),	℥
pound (Troy),	℔	package,	*pkg.*
pound sterling,	£	page,	*p*
Ledger,	*Led.*	pages,	*pp.*

paid,	*pd.*	September,	*Sept.*
pair,	*pr.*	share,	*sh.*
Pass Book,	*P. B.*	shipment,	*shipt.*
payment,	*payt.*	ship,	*sh.*
peck,	*pk.*	shipped,	*shipd*
pennyweight,	*pwt.*	sight,	*st.*
per cent,	*%*	south,	*S.*
Petty Cash Book,	*P. C. B.*	southeast,	*S. E.*
piece,	*pc.*	southwest,	*S. W.*
pint,	*pt.*	steamer,	*stmr.*
post office,	*P. O.*	steamship,	*stmp.*
post-office order,	*P. O. O.*	storage,	*stor.*
premium,	*prem.*	street,	*St.*
president (title),	*Pres.*	Sunday,	*Sun.*
professor (title),	*Prof.*	sundries,	*sunds.*
quart,	*qt.*	superfine,	*super.*
quarter,	*qr.*	superintendent (title),	*Supt.*
question (Is this right),	*?*	take (Med.),	℞
quire,	*qr.*	thousand,	*M.*
railroad,	*R. R.*	Thursday,	*Thurs..*
receipt,	*rect.*	transpose,	*tr.*
received,	*recd.*	treasurer,	*Treas.*
recording secretary,	*Rec. Sec.*	turn over; next page,	*T. O.*
reference (asterisk),	***	Tuesday,	*Tues.*
reverend (title),	*Rev.*	United States of America,	
Sales Book,	*S. B.*		*U. S. A.*
same,	" or *do.*	vessel,	*ves.*
Saturday,	*Sat.*	volume,	*vol.*
schooner,	*schr.*	Wednesday,	*Wed.*
seaport,	*spt.*	weight,	*wt.*
secretary,	*Sec.* or *Secty.*	west,	*W.*
seller's option,	*s. o.*	yard,	*yd.*
senator (title),	*Sen.*	year,	*yr.*
senior,	*Sr.*	yours,	*yrs.*

CHRISTIAN NAMES AND ABBREVIATIONS.
NAMES OF MEN.

Aaron	Constantine	Hector
Abel	Cornelius	Herbert
Abraham	Cyrus	Herman
Adam	Daniel, Dan.	Hiram
Alan	David	Horatio
Albert	Dennis	Hugh
Alexander, Alex.	Donald	Ignatius
Alfred, Alf.	Duncan	Ira
Allen	Edgar	Isaac
Alpheus	Edmund	Israel
Alvan	Edward, Edw.	Jacob
Amos	Eli	James, Jas.
Andrew	Elijah	Jasper
Archibald	Enoch	Jeremiah, Jer.
Arnold	Ephraim	Jesse
Arthur	Ernest	Job
Augustus	Ethan	Joel
Baldwin	Eugene	John, Jno.
Bartholomew	Everard	Jonathan, Jona.
Basil	Felix	Joseph, Jos.
Benedict	Ferdinand, Ferd.	Joshua
Benjamin, Benj.	Francis	Julian
Bernard	Frank	Julius, Jul.
Caleb	Franklin	Laurence
Calvin	Frederick, Fred.	Lawrence
Charles, Chas.	Gabriel	Levi
Christian	George, Geo.	Lewis
Christopher, Chr.	Gilbert	Louis
Claude	Godfrey	Luther
Clement	Gustavus	Marcus
Conrad	Harold	Mark

Martin	Patrick	Stephen
Matthew, Matt.	Paul	Theodore, Theo.
Maurice	Peter	Thomas, Thos.
Michael	Philip, Phil.	Timothy, Tim.
Morgan	Ralph	Tobias
Moses	Raphael	Ulysses
Nathan	Raymond	Uriah
Napoleon	Reuben	Valentine
Neal	Richard	Victor
Nicholas	Robert, Robt.	Vincent
Noah	Samuel, Saml.	Walter
Oliver	Sebastian	Washington
Orlando	Seth	Wesley
Oscar	Silas	West
Osmund	Simeon	William
Oswald	Simon	Zechariah, Zech.
Owen	Solomon	Zachary, Zach.

NAMES OF WOMEN.

Ada	Bertha	Dinah
Adelaide	Blanche	Dora
Adeline	Camilla	Dorcas
Agnes	Caroline	Dorothy
Alice	Catharine	Edith
Almira	Cecilia	Edna
Amanda	Celia	Eleanor
Amelia	Charlotte	Elinor
Amy	Chloe	Eliza
Ann	Christiana	Elizabeth
Anne	Clara	Ella
Augusta	Clarissa	Ellen
Barbara	Deborah	Elsie
Beatrice	Delia	Emma
Belle	Diana	Emeline

Emily	Juliana	Octavia
Ernestine	Juliet	Olivia
Esther	Katharine, Kate	Olympia
Eugenia	Laura	Pauline
Eugenie	Lena	Phebe
Eva	Letitia	Philippa
Evangeline	Leonora	Priscilla
Evelina	Lilian	Rachel
Fanny	Lilly	Rebecca
Felicia	Louisa	Rosa
Fidelia	Louise	Rosabella
Flora	Lucia	Rosalie
Florence	Lucinda	Rosamond
Frances	Lucretia	Ruth
Genevieve	Lydia	Sallie
Georgiana	Mabel	Sarah
Gertrude	Madeline	Selina
Grace	Magdalen	Sophia
Hannah	Magdalene	Stella
Harriet	Margaret	Susan
Helen	Maria	Susanna
Henrietta	Marianne	Tabitha
Hester	Martha	Theodora
Honora	Mary	Theodosia
Ida	Matilda	Thomasine
Irene	Maud	Valeria
Isabel	May	Victoria
Jane	Melicent	Vida
Janet	Minerva	Viola
Jeannette	Minnie	Violet
Jemima	Miranda	Virginia
Joan	Miriam	Vivian
Josephine	Nancy	Wilhelmina
Julia	Nora	Winifred

HOMOPHONES.

ale, a malt liquor.

ail, to trouble.

ate, did eat.

eight, twice four.

air, atmosphere.

heir, one who inherits.

all, every one.

awl, a small tool.

alter, to change.

altar, a communion table.

augur, to foretell.

auger, a carpenter's tool.

assent, consent.

ascent, upward movement.

adds, increases.

adz, a carpenter's tool.

annalist, a compiler of annals.

analyst, one who analyzes.

aught, anything.

ought, in duty bound.

ball, a round body.

bawl, to cry loudly.

bale, a large bundle.

bail, surety.

break, to part by force.

brake, means of stopping.

bare, uncovered.

bear, an animal.

be, to exist.

bee, an insect.

beech, a kind of tree.

beach, a seashore.

beet, a vegetable.

beat, to strike repeatedly.

breach, a break.

breech, the larger end of a gun.

bell, a hollow metallic vessel.

belle, a favorite lady.

berry, a kind of fruit.

bury, to cover, to inter.

bred, trained.

bread, food.

by, in care of, with, near.

buy, to purchase.

bored, pierced.

board, a thin plank.

borne, supported.

bourne, boundary.

bow, a knot.

beau, a lover.

broach, to open.

brooch, a breastpin.

blue, a color.

blew, did blow.

berth, a resting-place.

birth, nativity.

bow, to incline downward.

bough, a branch.

brows, arch over the eyes.

browse, to eat shrubs.

boll, the pod of a plant.

bowl, a drinking vessel.

candid, truthful.

candied, made like candy.

culler, one who culls.

color, hue or tint.

calender, to polish.

calendar, an almanac.

cannon, a large gun.

canon, a rule of doctrine.

canvass, to solicit.

canvas, a cotton cloth.

cast, to throw, to mold.

caste, social position.

caster, a cruet.

castor, a small wheel.

claws, talons.

clause, a part of a sentence.

cord, a small twine.

chord, a musical string.

cent, a copper coin.

scent, smell.

sent, did send.

course, a track.

coarse, rough, gross.

core, inner part.

corps, a body of troops.

cousin, a relative.

cozen, to deceive.

current, a stream.

currant, a kind of fruit.

draft, an order for money.

draught, a current of air.

deer, a kind of animal.

dear, beloved, costly.

discreet, cautious.

discrete, separate.

die, to lose life.

dye, to stain.

dew, atmospheric moisture.

due, payable.

dun, to attempt to collect.

done, performed, finished.

earn, to acquire by labor.

urn, a kind of vase.

fain, willingly.

feign, to pretend.

frays, quarrels.

phrase, a brief expression.

fare, food, price of passage.

fair, clear of blemish.

feet, plural of foot.

feat, performance.

flee, to run.

flea, an insect.

ferrule, a metallic band.

ferule, a kind of ruler.

find, to discover.

fined, sentenced to pay money.

fore, forward.

four, two and two.

fourth, the ordinal of four.

forth, forward.

flue, an exit.

flew, did fly.

fur, hair of certain animals.
fir, a kind of tree.
foul, impure.
fowl, a large edible bird.
gage, a fruit.
gauge, a measure.
gate, an entrance.
gait, manner of movement.
grate, a structure of bars.
great, large.
grater, a kind of rasp.
greater, larger.
guessed, supposed.
guest, a visitor.
gild, to overlay with gold leaf.
guild, an association.
grocer, trader in provisions.
grosser, more gross.
gilt, golden color.
guilt, crime.
grisly, frightful.
grizzly, somewhat gray.
gored, pierced by a horn.
gourd, a vegetable production.
groan, to moan.
grown, increased in size.
hale, healthy.
hail, frozen rain.
hare, a kind of animal.
hair, filaments growing from the skin.
hall, entrance.
haul, to pull.

herd, drove.
heard, did hear.
him, a pronoun.
hymn, a sacred song.
heel, part of the foot.
heal, to cure.
hear, to perceive by the ear.
here, in this place.
hole, a cavity.
whole, entire.
hue, color.
hew, to cut as with an ax.
lade, to load.
laid, placed.
leaf, foliage.
lief, willingly.
led, conducted.
lead, a kind of metal.
lessen, to make less.
lesson, something to be learned.
lie, a willful falsehood.
lye, an alkaline solution.
lone, solitary.
loan, permission to use.
made, finished.
maid, unmarried woman.
male, masculine.
mail, to post.
mane, hair on the neck of certain animals.
main, chief.
Maine, the name of a State.

mantle, a cloak.

mantel, a chimney shelf.

marshal, to put in order.

martial, warlike.

mean, stingy, low-minded.

mien, manner.

miner, worker in a mine.

minor, under legal age.

mite, a minute object.

might, power.

mist, fine rain.

missed, did miss.

moan, audible grief.

mown, cut down.

mode, manner.

mowed, cut with a mower.

nay, no.

neigh, to whinny.

need, urgent want.

knead, to work into a mass.

nap, a short sleep.

knap, the fuzz of cloth.

night, between dusk and dawn.

knight, a champion.

no, a denial.

know, to understand.

nose, part of the face.

knows, understands.

oh, an exclamation.

owe, to be indebted to.

ore, unrefined metal.

oar, a long paddle.

o'er, a contraction of over.

our, belonging to us.

hour, sixty minutes.

pale, of light tint.

pail, a bucket.

pane, a division of glass.

pain, uneasy feeling.

plane, a woodworker's tool.

plain, without ornament.

plate, a vessel to eat from.

plait, a fold.

pray, request earnestly.

prey, plunder, booty.

pare, to cut off the rind.

pair, a couple.

pear, a kind of fruit.

paws, feet of a beast.

pause, a stop or rest.

piece, a part.

peace, quietude.

peak, the topmost point.

pique, resentment.

peel, the covering of fruit.

peal, a ringing sound.

pier, a wharf.

peer, equal in rank.

please, delight.

pleas, legal answers.

pendant, that which hangs.

pendent, hanging.

pole, a slender piece of wood.

poll, the head.

pore, a minute interstice.

pour, to cause to flow.

plum, a fruit.

plumb, the weight on a plumbline.

profit, to gain.   [tells.

prophet, one who fore-

pearl, a shelly concretion.

purl, murmur.

quire, twenty-four sheets of paper.

choir, company of singers.

quarts, plural of quart.

quartz, a mineral.

rain, water from the clouds.

reign, to rule.

rein, part of a bridle.

rays, beams of light.

raise, to lift up.

raze, to demolish.

rap, to knock.

wrap, to envelop.

reed, the stem of a plant.

read, to peruse.

red, a color.

read, did read.

rest, to repose.

wrest, to take violently.

retch, to feel like vomiting.

wretch, miserable person.

rite, a ceremony.

right, correct.

wright, a workman.

write, to form letters.

roe, the eggs of a fish.

row, a line or rank.

rye, a kind of grain.

wry, crooked.

ring, a circle.

wring, to twist.

seed, that which produces.

cede, to yield or surrender.

shown, revealed.

shone, did shine.

sleight, dexterity.

slight, slender.

so, in that manner.

sow, to scatter grain.

sew, to fasten by stitches.

seller, one who sells.

cellar, underground room.

sold, did sell.

soled, provided with a sole.

seen, perceived by the eye.

scene, a view.

sale, the act of selling.

sail, a ship's canvas.

sailor, a mariner.

sailer, a boat which sails.

steak, a slice of fresh meat.

stake, to mark the limits.

steel, a kind of metal.

steal, to take unlawfully.

sweet, pleasing to the senses.

suite, attendants.

sole, single.

soul, the immortal part.

sore, tender to the touch.

soar, to fly upward.

skull, head bone.

scull, impel with one oar.

sum, the amount.

some, an indefinite quantity.

sun, a center of light.

son, a male descendant.

tale, a narrative.

tail, posterior extremity.

tare, a deduction of weight.

tear, to rend.

their, belonging to them.

there, at that place.

tacks, small nails.

tax, a public assessment.

teem, to produce abundantly.

team, those employed together.

tear, water from the eye.

tier, a row or rank.

teas, plural of tea.

tease, to annoy.

the, a limiting word.

thee, objective case of thou.

tide, current.

tied, fastened.

time, duration.

thyme, an herb.

throw, to hurl.

throe, anguish.

throne, a royal seat.

thrown, hurled.

toe, part of the foot.

tow, to pull.

told, did tell.

tolled, rung slowly.

toll, a tax.

tole, induce to follow.

to, in the direction of.

too, also.

two, twice one.

threw, did throw.

through, to the end.

tun, a cask.

ton, a measure of weight.

vain, ineffectual.

vein, a blood vessel.

vane, a weathercock.

vial, a small bottle.

viol, a musical instrumer'

vice, wickedness.

vise, a kind of press.

wade, to walk in water.

weighed, tested by balance.

waste, to lose.

waist, part of the body.

wait, to stay.

weight, pressure.

wave, an undulation.

waive, to relinquish.

way, a road.

weigh, to test by balance.

ware, articles of trade.

wear, to have on the body

week, seven days.

weak, deficient in strength.

wood, timber.

would, past tense of will.

WORDS WHICH ARE NEARLY HOMOPHONOUS.

ab o li tion, an annulling.

  eb ul li tion, a bubbling.

ac cept, to receive or admit.

  ex cept, to leave out.

ac cess, admittance.

  ex cess, more than suf-
ficient.

af fect, to influence.

  ef fect, result.

ar rant, gross, flagrant.

  er rant, roving.

  er rand, mission.

as say, to try.

  es say, endeavor.

bea con, a signal fire.

  beck on, to call by a sign.

borne, conveyed, carried.

  born, brought forth.

brood, to think anxiously.

  brewed, did brew.

boo ty, pillage, plunder.

  beau ty, loveliness.

bile, fluid from the liver.

  boil, a kind of tumor.

bust, a piece of sculpture.

  burst, to open violently.

car at, a twenty-fourth part.

  ca ret, a mark (∧).

  car rot, a vegetable.

cap i tal, first in import-
ance.

  cap i tol, a statehouse.

choose, to prefer.

  chews, grinds with the
teeth.

close, to conclude, to stop.

  clothes, clothing.

cloth, a woven fabric.

  clothe, to apparel.

coal, a kind of fuel.

  cold, deprived of heat.

con cur, to agree.

  con quer, to overpower.

cor po ral, relating to the
body.   [body.

  cor po re al, having a

cur ri er, one who dresses
leather.

  cou ri er, a public mes-
senger.

de cent, proper, decorous.

  de scent, slope, lineage.

  dis sent, disagree.

de sert, to leave.

  des sert, a dinner course
of sweetmeats.

def er ence, honor.

  dif fer ence, disagree-
ment.

dome, an arched roof.

  doom, condemnation.

di lu tion, act of making
thin or weak.

  de lu sion, false belief.

dire, dreadful.

dy er, one who colors cloth.

dis ease, sickness.

de cease, death.

ear, the organ of hearing.

year, twelve months.

em i nent, distinguished.

im mi nent, impending.

e lic it, to deduce.

il lic it, prohibited.

e lude, to avoid.

il lude, to disappoint.

e rup tion, a bursting out.

ir rup tion, a bursting in.

ex or cise, to adjure.

ex er cise, practice.

ei ther, one of two.

e ther, a kind of fluid.

ex e cu ter, one who executes.

ex ec u tor, one who performs the will of another.

ha lo, a luminous circle.

hal low, to sanctify.

hal loo, to shout, to call.

ha ven, a place of safety.

heav en, abode of bliss.

hire, salary.

high er, taller.

ho ly, pure.

whol ly, totally.

i dol, a false god.

i dle, indolent.

im po tent, powerless.

im pu dent, insulting.

in sight, inspection.

in cite, to provoke.

in ge ni ous, inventive.

in gen u ous, artless.

jest, a joke.

just, proper, true, legal.

line, a cord; a succession.

loin, a part of the back.

lin ea ment, outline.

lin i ment, a fluid ointment.

light ning, atmospheric electricity.

light en ing, making lighter.

loath, reluctant.

loathe, to hate.

lore, knowledge.

low er, to let down.

li ar, a deceiver.

lyre, a kind of harp.

ma, a contraction of mamma.

mar, to spoil.

mash, to crush.

mesh, an opening in a net.

marsh, a swamp.

mes sage, an errand.

mas sage, a rubbing of the body.

me ter, that which measures.

me te or, a fiery body.

mis sile, a projectile.

mis le, a thick mist.

more, a greater quantity.

mow er, a machine.

moun tain, a very high elevation of earth.

mount ing, going up.

mus lin, thin cotton cloth.

muz zling, covering the mouth.

nei ther, not the one or the other.

neth er, under.

pa, a contraction of papa.

par, equal value.

pet ri fac tion, conversion into stone.

pu tre fac tion, offensive decay.

pil low, a cushion.

pil lar, that which supports.

pop u lace, people.

pop u lous, well settled.

pom ace, ground fruit.

pum ice, a kind of cinder.

rad ish, a vegetable.

red dish, somewhat red.

rare, not frequent.

rear, to raise.

real, actual.

reel, to wind.

rel ic, that which remains.

rel ict, a widow.

rid i cule, to expose to laughter.

ret i cule, a little bag.

roar, a loud continuous sound.

row er, one who rows.

serge, a kind of cloth.

surge, to roll as a wave.

set, to place, to locate.

sit, to rest, to seat.

shore, a beach.

sure, doubtless.

soar, to fly upward.

sow er, one who sows.

sought, did seek.

sort, quality.

stat ute, a law.

stat ue, a carved image.

stalk, a stem.

stork, a kind of bird.

sur plus, excess.

sur plice, official robe of a clergyman.

sym bol, a sign.   [ment.

cym bal, a musical instru-

track, a path or mark.

tract, a district, an essay.

through, from end to end.

thor ough, complete.

taught, did teach.

taut, stretched tightly.

yarn, woollen thread.

yearn, to grieve.

yoke, to couple together.

yolk, yellow of an egg.

WORD FORMATIONS FROM ORIGINAL ROOTS.

actum (L.) = to do;
+ive, +ion, +ivity, +uary, +uate, en+, trans+, re+ion.

arche (G.) = beginning, government, chief;
(1)   (2)   (3)
(1)   (1)   (2   (3)   (3)   (3)
+etype, +eology, an+y, +itect, +bishop, +angel, patri+.

annus (L.) = year;
+als, +ual, +uity, +iversary, semi+ual, super+uated.

arma (L.) = arms or weapons;
+s, +y, +istice, +ory, fore+, re+, dis+, un+ed.

audio (L.) = to hear;
+ble, +bly, +ence, +t, +tor, +torium, in+ble.

autos (G.) = one's self;
+biography, +type, +psy, +graph, +matic, +crat, +harp.

bene (L.) = well;
*fit, *ficial, *factor, *volence, *diction.

biblos (G.) = book;
+e, +iography, +iomania, +iolatry, +iotheca.

cado (L.) = to fall;
+dence, +sual, cas+de, de+dence, de+y, oc+sion.

(1)   (1)   (2)
caedo (L.) = to cut, to kill;
(1)   (1)   (1)   (1) ·   (2)   (2)
con+se, pre+se, ex+se, in+sion, homi+de, sui+de.

caput (L.) = head;
+ital, +itation, +itulate, re+itulate, de+itate, +tain.

(1)   (2)
cedo (L.) = to yield, to go;
(1) (1) (2) (1) (1) (2) (2) (2)
+e, re+e, ac+e, con+e, pre+e, inter+e, ante+ent, pre+ent.

centum (L.) = hundred;
+s, +ury, +enarian, +ennial, +iped, per+age.

cheir (G.) = hand;
+ography, +ology, +omancy, +opody, +ogymnast.

chronos (G.) = time;
+icle, +ograph, +ography, +ology, +ometer, +oscope.

6

     (1) (2) (3)
citum (L.) = to summon, rouse, cite ;
 (1) (2) (2)   (2)   (2) (3) (3)
+ e, ex + e, in + e, in + ement, resus + ate, re + e, re + ation.

circus (L.) = circle ;
 + le, + let, en + le, semi + le, + ular, + ulate, + uit, + us.

civis (L.) = citizen ;
 + ty, + tizen, + vil, + vilian, + vilize, un + vil, un + vilized.

clamo (L.) = to speak loudly ;
 + or, ac + ation, de + ation, ‖ **claim;** ex*, re*, dis*, pro*.

claudo (L.) = to shut ;
 + ose, + oset, + ause, + oister, in + ude, con + ude, ex + ude,
 se + ude, pre + ude.

cultum (L.) = to cultivate ;
 + ivate, + ure, agri + ure, horti + ure, flori + ure.

cor (L.) = heart ;
 *e, *dial, con*d, con*dance, dis*d, re*d, re*ded.

corpus (L.) = body ;
 + s, + se, + oral, + oration, + oreal, + ulent, in + orate.

credo (L.) = believe ;
 + ence, + ential, + ible, in + ible, in + ulity, + it, + itor, dis + it.

creo (L.) = create ;
 + ate, + ature, + ative, + ator, re + ate, re + ation, mis + ant.

cretum (L.) = grow ;
 con + te, ex + scence, de + ase, in + ase.

cumbo (L.) = lie down ;
 en + er, en + rance, in + ent, re + ent, pro + ent, suc + .

cura (L.) = care ;
 + e, + able, + ate, + iosity, pro + e, se + ity, sine + e.

curro (L.) = run ;
 + rency, + rent, con + , dis + sive, ex + sion, oc + , re + rence.

debeo (L.) = owe ;
 + t, + tor, + it, in + ted, in + tedness, + enture.

decem (L.) = ten ;
 + imal, + imate, + ember, + ade, + ennial, duo + imo.

demos (G.) = people ;
 + agogue, + ocrat, + ocracy, epi + ic, epi + ics.

dens (L.) = tooth ;
 + t, + ts, in + t, in + ture, in + tation, + tist, + tistry, + tifrice.

dico (L.) = say ;

+ tion, + tionary, + tate, + tator, bene + tion, contra + t, e + t, in + t, inter + t, male + tion, pre + t, pre + ate, ver + t.

dies (L.) = day ;

+ ary, + urnal, + al, meri + an (M.), antemeri + an (A. M.), postmeri + an (P. M.).

doceo (L.) = teach ;

+ tor, + trine, + ument, + uments, + ile, + ility.

(1)   (2)
domus (L.) = house ;   **dormio** (L.) = to sleep ;

(1)   (1)   (1)   (2   (2)   (2)   (2)
+ e, + esticate, + icile ; + ant, antly, + itory, + er window.

doxa (G.) = opinion ;

+ ology, ortho +, hetero +, para +, para + ical.

duco (L.) = to lead ;

+ t, + tile, ab + t, aque + t, con + t, con + e, de + t, de + e, e + e, e + ate, in + e, intro + e, pro + e, re + e, tra + e.

(e)
æquus (L.) = just, equal.

+ al, + able, + ation, + ator, + ilibrium, + inox, + ity, + ivalent, + ivocate, un + ivocal, + ality, in + ality.

(1)   (2)
facio (L.) = to do, to make ;

(1)   (1)   (1)   (1)   (2)
+ t, + tor, + tion, + tious, + ulty.

(1)   (2)
fendo, fensum (L.) = strike ;

(1)   (1)   (1)   (1)   (2)   (2)   (2)   (2)
+ er, de +, de + ant ; of +, de + e, de + ive, of + e, of + ive,

(2)
inof + ive.

fero (L.) = carry ;

+ ry, + tile, of +, suf +, con +, de +, dif +, in +, trans +, re +.

fido (L.) = trust ;

+ elity, con + e, con + ence, dif + ence, in + el, per + y

finis (L.) = limit ;

+ ish, + ite, in + ite, de + ite, de + ition, con + e, con + es.

firmus (L.) = strong ;

+ er, + ament, af +, af + ation, con +, in +, in + ity, in + ary.

fluo (L.) = flow ;

+ ent, + id, + ctuate, af + ent, con + ence, in + ence, super + ity.

forma (L.) = form ;
　+s, +al, +ation, +ula, con+, de+, in+, per+, re+, trans+,
　uni+.

fractum (L.) = break ;
　+ion, +ious, +ure, in+ion, re+ion, re+ive, re+ory.

fusum (L.) = pour ;
　+e, +ion, con+ion, dif+e, dif+ion, ef+ion, in+e, pro+e,
　trans+e, suf+e.

ge (G.) = earth ;
　*ography, *ology, *ometry, *ocentric, *odesy.

genitum (L.) = produce ;
　+ial, con+ial, +ius, in+ious, +eral, +der, en+der, +tle,
　+tile, +erate, de+erate, re+erate, pro+itor, primo+iture.

　　(1)　　　　　　　　(2)
grapho (G.) = write ;　**gram**ma = writing ;
　(1)　(1)　　(1)　　　(1)　　　(1)　　(2)　　(2)　　(2)
　+ic, +ite, para+, steno+y, tele+ ; +mar, dia+, ana+.

　　　　　(1)　　(2)
gratus (L.) = thankful, agreeable ,
　(1)　　(1)　　(1)　　　(2)　　　(2)　　(2)　　(2)
　+eful, +itude, in+itude, in+iate, +uitous, +ify, con+ulate.

junctum (L.) = join ;
　+ion, +ure, ad+, con+ure, con+ion, dis+ion, in+ion,
　sub+ive.

jus (L.) = right ;
　*t, un*t, *tice, in*tice, *tify, un*tifiable, +rist, +risdiction.

　(1)　　(2)
lego, lectum (L.) = read ;
　(1)　　(2)　　(2)　　(2)　　(2)　　(2)　　(2)　　(2)
　+ible, +ure, dia+, e+, col+, recol+, se+, intel+.

legis (L.) = law ;
　+al, il+al, +alize, +itimate, +islature, privi+e, il+itimate.

litera (L.) = letter ;
　*ture, *ry, il*te, ob*te, al*tion, *l, *lly.

logos (G.) = speech ;
　+ic, +ical, ana+y, apo+y, philo+y, cata+ue, dia+ue.

　　(1)　　　(2)
loquor, **locut**us (L.) = speak ;
　(1)　　(1)　　(1)　　　(2)　　　(2)
　+acity, e+ent, col+ial, circum+ion, e+ion.

luo (L.) = wash ;
  ab + tion, al + vial, antedi + vian, di + te, di + tion, pol + te.

(1)   (2)
magnus (L.) = great ; **major** (L.) = greater ;
  (1)   (1)   (1)   (1)   (2)   (2)
  + itude, + ify, + animous, + ificence ; *ity, * general.

malus (L.) = bad ;
  + ice, + ign, + ignant, + aria, + practice, + content.

manus (L.) = hand ;
  + al, + facture, + mit, + mission, + script, a + ensis.

merz (L.) = wares, traffic ;
  + chant, + chandise, + cantile, + cenary, + cer, com + ce.

(1)   (2)   (3)
metior, mensus (L.) = to measure ; **metron** (G.) = measure ;
  (1)   (1)   (2)   (2)   (3)   (3)
  + asure, ad + asurement, + uration, im + e ; + er, dia + er.

migro (L.) = to change residence ;
  + ate, + ation, + atory, e + ate, e + ant, im + ate, trans + ate.

minor (L.) = less ;
  *ity, + iature, + ute, + us, + ion, + uend, + utia, di + utive.

(1)   (2)
mitto, missum (L.) = to send ;
  (1)   (1)   (1)   (1)   (2)   (2)   (2)
  ad +, com +, sub +, re +, + ile, + ion, ad + ion, com + ion,
      (2)   (2)   (2)   (2)   (2)   (2)
  dis +, manu + ion, + ive, per + ion, pro + ory, re +.

modus (L.) = manner or form ;
  + e, + el, + ify, + ulate, + eration, + esty, com + ious, com + ity,
  accom + ate, unaccom + ating, incom + e, ala + e.

monos (G.) = alone ;
  + k, + astery, + arch, + ogram, + opolize, + osyllable, + otony.

munus (L.) = office or gift ;
  + icipal, + ificence, com + e, com + icate, com + ity, com + ion,
  excom + icate, im + ity, re + erate, unre + erative.

nastus (L.) = to be born ;
  + al, + ive, + ion, + ural, preter + ural, super + ural, in + e.

nomen (L.) = name ;
  + inal, + inate, de + inate, *clature, mis + er, ig + iny.

notum (L.) = know ;
  + e, + ed, + ing, + ion, + ice, + ify, + ation, de + e.

opus (L.) = work ;
  +erate, +erator, +era, co+erate, in+perative.
ora (L.) = to pray ;
  *tion, *tor, *cle, *l, ad*ble, ex*ble, inex*ble.
orthos (G.) = correct ;
  +dox, +epy, +graphy, +scope.
pan (G.) = all ;
  *acea, *egyric, *oply, *orama, *tomime, *-American.
partis (L.) = part ;
  +ner, +y, +icle, +icular, +icipate, +isan, +ition, +ial,
  im+ial, a+ment, com+ment, de+ment, im+, bi+ite.
pater (L.) = father ;
  *nal, +iot, com+iot, +iarch, +on, +ician, ex+iate.
(1)   (2)
pello, pulsum (L.) = to drive ;
  (1)   (1)   (1)   (1)   (1)   (1)   (2)   (2)   (2)
  com+, dis+, ex+, im+, pro+, re+ ; +e, com+ion, im+e,
  (2)
  re+e.
(1)   (2)
pendeo (L.) = to hang; **pendo** = to weigh ;
  (1)   (1)   (1)   (1)   (1)   (1)   (1)   (2)   (2)
  +ant, +ent, +ulum, ap+, de+, im+, sus+ ; ex+, com+
        (1)
(pes) pedis (L.) = foot ;
  (1)   (1)   (1)   (1)   (1)   (1)   (1)
  +al, +estal, +dle, +igree, ex+ient, im+e, ex+ite.
(1)   (2)
pleo (L.) = to fill; **plenus** (L.) = full ;
  (1)   (1)   (1)   (1)   (1)   (2)   (2)
  com+te, de+te, ex+tive, re+te, sup+ment; +ty, +itude.
plico (L.) = to fold or twist ;
  ap+ation, com+ate, du+ate, im+ate, ex+it, im+it.
positum (L.) = to place ;
  +ion, com+ion, op+ion, ex+ion, pre+ion, trans+ion.
primus (L.) = first ;
  +e, +er, +ary, +rose, +itive, +ogeniture, +ate, +eval.
privus (L.) = private ;
  +ate, +acy, +ilege, +ation. +ateer, de+e.
rectus (L.) = right ;
  +itude, +ify, cor+, di+, indi+, +ilinear.

ruptum (L.) = to break;
+ ure, ab+, bank+, cor+, dis+, e+, ir+, inter+.

(1)   (2)
scribo, scriptum (L.) = to write or draw;
(1) + e, as + e, circum + e, de + e, in + e, pre + e, pro + e, sub + e;
(2) + ure, as + ion, de + ion, pre + ion, pro + ion, sub + ion.

(1)   (2)
servo (L.) = to watch, preserve;
(1) (1) (1) (1) (1) (1) (2) (2) (2)
+ ant, + ice, + ile, de + e, ob + e, sub + e, pre + e, con + e, re + oir.

stenos (G.) = narrow, close, or little;
+ graph, + graphy, + grapher, + graphic.

specio (L.) = to see;
+ tacle, + imen, + ify, a + t, in + t, per + tive, pro + t, re + t.

spiro (L.) = to breathe;
+ it, + itual, a + e, con + e, ex + e, in + e, per + e, tran + e.

structum (L.) = to build;
+ ure, con +, de + ion, in +, ob +, super + ure.

super (L.) = above;
*ior, *lative, *b, *natural, *numerary, *scribe.

tendo (L.) = to extend;
+ ency, at +, con +, dis +, ex +, in +, por +, pre +, superin +.

teneo (L.) = to hold;
+ ure, + ant, + ement, + et, + on, + or, con + ts, con + tment, de + tion, lieu + ant, re + tive, coun + ance, main + ance, sus + ance.

testis (L.) = witness;
+ s, + ed, + ify, + ament, + ator, + imony, at +, con +, de +, pro +, pro + ant.

traho (L.) = to draw;
+ in, + ce, + ct, + ction, abs + ct, at + ct, con + ct, de + ct, ex + ct, pro + ct, re + ct, sub + ct, sub + hend, por + y, por + it.

usus (L.) = to use;
+ e, + age, + ual, + ury, + urp, ab + e, mis + e, per + e.

valeo (L.) = to have strength, force or value;
+ iant, + id, + or, + ue, in + id, in + uable, pre + ent.

venic (L.) = to come;
+ ture, a + ue, re + ue, con + t, con + tion, e + t, in + t, pre + t.

(1) (2)
verto, versum (L.) = to turn;

(1) (1) (1) (1) (1) (1) (1) (1) (2)
a+, ad+, ad+ise, con+, di+, in+, per+, re+, sub+; ad+e,

(2) (2) (2) (2) (2) (2) (2) (2)
con+e, di+e, in+e, per+e, ob+e, re+e, sub+ive, trans+e.

via (L.) = way;

de*te, ob*te, *duct, tri*l.

(1) (2)
video, visum (L.) = to see;

(1) (1) (2) (2) (2) (2) (2)
e+ent, pro+ent; +ion, +ible, +it, +age, +ta.

(1) (2)
voco, vocatum (L.) = to call;

(1) (1) (1) (2) (2)
+ation, +al, +abulary; ad+e, equi+e, pro+ion.

volvo (L.) = to roll or to fold;

+ume, +uble, e+ve, in+ve, re+ve, re+ution, circum+ution.

WORD FORMATIONS BY THE USE OF PREFIXES.

(1) (2) (3)
a = on, at, toward;

(1) (1) (1) (1) (2) (3) (3)
*bed, *board, *loft, *ground, *broad, *back, *baft.

(1) (2)
ab = from, abandon;

(1) (1) (1) (1) (2)
*duct, *stract, *scond, *breviate, *dicate.

(1) (2) (3) (4) (5) (6) (7) (8) (9) (10)
ad, ac-, af-, ag-, al-, an-, ap-, ar-, as-, at-, = to;

(1) *duce, *here, *jacent, *mit, *vent, *verse, *vertise.

(2) *cede, *cord, *cept, *cess, *claim, *count, *commodate.

(3) *fable, *fect, *filiate, *firm, *flict, *front, *fluence.

(4) *glutinate, *grandize, *gravate, *grieve, *gress, *itate.

(5) *lay, *ly, *lot, *low, *lure, *lude, *literation.

(6) *archy, *ecdote, *nex, *nounce, *noy, *nul, *notate.

(7) *pall, *paratus, *parel, *parent, *peal, *pear, *pease,
  *plause, *preciate, *proach, *prove, *propriate,
  *proximate.

(8) *raign, *range, *ray, *rear, *rest, *rive, *rogate.

(9) *rend, *certain, *perse, *pirate, *sault, *sess, *sign,
  *sociate, *sort, *sure, *similate, *sist, *sert.

(10) *tach, *tack, *tain, *tempt, *tend, *test, *tract, *tune.

ana = anew, against, similar to.

(1) (2) (3)

*baptist, *chronism, *logy.

(1) (2) (3)

ante = before ;

*cedent, *chamber, *date, *diluvian, *meridian, *mundane.

anti = opposite ;

*-American, *christian, *climax, *friction, *pode, *pathy, *septic, *type, + arctic, + acid, + agonize, + alkaline, + asthmatic.

bi = two ;

*as, *angular, *centennial, *cuspid, *cycle, *ennial, *monthly, *partite, *ped, *valve, *weekly.

circum = around ;

*ference, *fuse, *locution, *navigate, *rotary, *scribe, *spection, *stance, *vention, *volution.

con = with or together ;

*cede, *centric, *cert, *clude, *cord, *cur, *federate, *ference, *fess, *form, *genial, *gress, *sign, *stitution, *tort, *tract, *vention, *vivial, *voke, *vey, + act, + adjutant, + agent, + agulate, + alition, + ercion, + eval, + exist, + here, + operate, + ordinate, + partnership.

contra = against ;

*band, *dict, *distinguish, *vene, *ry, + alto.

de = from or down ;

*bar, *bate, *bauch, *bilitate, *camp, *cay, *cease, *ceive, *cide, *cline, *duct, *fault, *form, *grade, *ject, *light, *liver, *lude, *monstrate, *moralize, *mur, *pend, *populate, *press, *scend, *tract, *volve.

dis = separation ;

*agree, *ease, *order, *use, *band, *grace, *like, *lodge, *member, *miss, *mount, *robe, *ruption, *solve.

(1) (2)

ex = out, beyond ;

(1) *act, *claim, *clude, *communicate, *coriate, *crescence, *cruciating, *cursion, *empt, *ercise, *ert, *hale, *hibit, *ile, *ist, *odus, *pand, *pect, *pend, *plain, *plode, *pose, *press, *punge, *tant, *tend, *terior, *tinguish, *ult, *-president.

(2) *aggerate, *alt, *asperate, *ceed, *cess, *orbitant, *tra.

extra – beyond or outside;
*judicial, *mundane, *-official, *ordinary, *s.

fore = before;
*cast, *close, *father, *hand, *head, *judge, *knowledge,
*man, *see, *show, *stall, *taste, + ward, *-topmast.

(1)   (2)   (3)   (4)   (a) (b)
in (im), en (em) – in, not;
(1a) *carnate, *case, *centive, *come, *close, *dorse.
(1b) *active, *animate, *applicable, *attention, *capable.
(2a) *bank, *bed, *bibe, *bitter, *bosom, *burse.
(2b) *material, *mature, *measurable, *movable.
(3a) *cage, *chain, *chant, *circle, *compass, *fold, *trance.
(4a) *balm, *bank, *bark, *bosom, *boss, *brace, *broil.

inter – between;
*cede, *cept, *communication, *est, *fere, *im, *line, *lude,
*mediate, *mittent, *national, *pose, *rogate, *rupt, *sect,
*stice, *vene, *view, *weave.

mis – wrong, wrongly or ill;
*apply, *arrange, *become, *believe, *carriage, *calculate,
*construe, *doing, *fortune, *judge, *name, *rule, *state,
*take, *trust, *understand, †use.

out = beyond the limits;
*cast, *do, *doors, *grow, *look, *post, *rank, *run, *sell,
*shine, *side, *ward, *weigh, *wind, *work.

(1)   (2)   (3)   (4)
over = above, excess, beyond, across;
(1) *alls, *arch, *cast, *head, *lay, *shadow, *spread.
(2) *act, *care, *charge, *estimate, *dose, *due, *work.
(3) *board, *climb, *flow, *grow, *hang. (4) *land, *sea.

pre = before;
*amble, *caution, *cede, *clude, *conceive, *concerted,
*destine, *disposed, *dominate, *eminent, *exist, *face,
*fer, *fix, *judge, *lude, *meditated, *mium, *occupy,
*pare, *scription, *sent, *tend, *vent.

pro = before or forward;
*blem, *boscis, *ceed, *digal, *digy, *duce, *fane, *fess,
*found, *genitor, *gramme, *hibit, *ject, *lific, *lix,
*long, *menade, *mote, *nounce, *pel, *pose, *scribe,
*tect, *test, *tract, *verb, *vide, *voke, *vost.

(1)   (2)
re = again, back ;

(1) *act, *address, *adjust, *admit, *affirm, *arrange, *assure, *claim, *commence, *construct, *deem, *examine, *generate, *produce, *search, *solve, *spond, *sume.

(2) *bound, *cant, *cede, *cline, *coil, *cur, *lapse, *pose.

(1) (2) (3) (4) (5)
sub (suc, suf, sum, sup) = under ;

(1) *agent, *altern, *aqueous, *-base, *-bass, *committee, *cutaneous, *deacon, *delegate, *divide, *due, *editor, *ject, *jugate, *lime, *marine, *merge, *mission, *ordinate, *scribe, *side, *sist, *stance, *stitute, *terfuge, *tile, *tle, *tract, *urb, *vert.

(2) *ceed, *cess, *cessor, *cinct, *cor, *cumb.

(3) *fer, *fice, *ficient, *fix, *focate, *frage, *fuse.

(4) *s, *mary, *mit, *mon, *mons.

(5) *plant, *plement, *plicate, *ply, *port, *pose, *press.

(1) (2) (3)
super (sur, sus) = over or above;

(1) *abundance, *add, *annuate, *cilious, *ficial, *fine, *fluity, *human, *induce, *intend, *ior, *natural, *numerary, *scription, *sede, *stition, *struction.

(2) *cease, *charge, *cingle, *feit, *mise, *mount, *name, *plus, *prise, *render, *round, *vey, *vive.

(3) *ceptible, re*citate, *pect, *pend, *pender, *pense, *tain.

trans = across or over ;

*act, *atlantic, *cend, *cript, *fer, *figure, *fix, *form, *fuse *gress, *it, *late, *location, *lucent, *migrate, *mission, *mit, *mute, *om, *parent, *pire, *plant, *port, *pose.

tri = three ;

*angle, *centenary, *color, *lateral, *o, *pthong, *ple, *une.

un = not ;

*able, *belief, *concern, *divided, *faithful, *gainly, *happy, *interested, *known, *lovely, *natural, *righteous, *sealed *warranted, *written, *wind.

under = beneath ;

*current, *go, *graduate, *hand, *lay, *pinning, *shirt, *tenant, *tone, *value, *wear, *writer.

vice = second in rank ;

*regent, *roy, * admiral, * consul, * president.

WORD FORMATIONS BY THE USE OF SUFFIXES.

Suffixes assist in forming nouns (N.), adjectives (A.), adverbs (Ad.), and verbs (V.):

able = capable of being (A.);
 change+, consol+, teach+, mov+, justifi+.

ac = (1) pertaining to (A.); (2) one who (N.);
 (1) cardi+, demoni+, elegi+ ; (2) mani+.

aceous = having the nature of (A.);
 aren+, argill+, capill+, foli+, sapon+.

acious = having the nature of (A.);
 aud+, effic+, sag+, fall+, pugn+, bib+.

acy = (1) state of being; (2) quality of being (N.);
 (1) celib+, lun+, legitim+ ; (2) effic+, fall+, delic+.

age = (1) that which; (2) condition of being; (3) collection
 of (N.);
 (1) assembl+, carri+ ; (2) orphan+ ; (3) foli+, cord+

al = belonging to (A.);
 magic+, music+, regiment+, voc+, rur+.

an = (1) one who (N.); (2) pertaining to (A.);
 (1) Baltimore+, Europe+ ; (2) epicure+, republic+.

ant = (1) one who; (2) that which (N.); (3) state of being (A.);
 (1) assist+, assail+ ; (2) conson+, quadr+ ; (3) luxuri+.

ance = (1) state of being; (2) act of (N.);
 (1) abund+, disturb+, deliver+ ; (2) admitt+, resist+.

ar = (1) one who; (2) that which; (3) like; (4) relating to;
 (1) schol+ ; (2) coll+ ; (3) globul+ ; (4) ocul+, sol+.

ard = one who (N.);
 drunk+, lagg+, bragg+, cow+.

ary = (1) place where; (2) one who; (3) that which (N.);
 (4) pertaining to (A.);
 (1) gran+, infirm+ ; (2) secret+ ; (3) bound+ ; (4)
 element+, culin+.

ate = (1) act of (V.); (2) one who; (3) that which (N.);
 (1) abbrevi+, emigr+ ; (2) magistr+, pir+ ; (3) opi+.

atic = (1) pertaining to (A.); (2) one who (N.);
 (1) aqu+, emblem+, asthm+, rheum+ ; (2) lun+, fan+.

cle = small (N.);
arti+, carbun+, parti+, folli+, ici+, pinna+.

cule = (1) small; (2) minute (N.);
(1) reti+ ; (2) animal+, mole+.

d = past time (V.);
confide+, deride+, reside+, subside+, transcribe+.

dom = (1) territory of; (2) condition or state of being (N.);
(1) Christen+, king+, duke+; (2) martyr+, free+, wis+.

ed = past time (V.);
gain+, honor+, join+, laud+, mann+, play+.

ee = one to whom (N.);
assign+, grant+, patent+, pay+, refer+, trust+.

eer = one who (N.);
auction+, pion+, engin+, volunt+, mountain+.

en = (1) to make (V.); (2) made of (A.); (3) small (N.);
(1) black+, length+ ; (2) earth+, wood+ ; (3) chick+,
maid+, gard+.

ence = (1) quality of being; (2) condition of being; (3) place
where (N.);
(1) dilig+, prud+ ; (2) opul+ ; (3) resid+.

ency = (1) quality of being; (2) office of; (3) place where;
(4) that which (N.);
(1) profici+ ; (2) presid+ ; (3) ag+ ; (4) curr+.

ent = (1) having the quality of (A.); (2) one who; (3) that
which (N.);
(1) depend+, dilig+ ; (2) superintend+ ; (3) anteced+.

er = (1) more (A.); (2) one who; (3) that which (N.);
(1) fond+, dear+ ; (2) teach+, sing+ ; (3) reap+,
mow+, vouch+.

ern = belonging to (A.);
east+, north+, south+, west+, mod+, patt+.

ery = (1) place where; (2) collection of; (3) art of (N.);
(1) fish+, rook+, nurs+ ; (2) confection+ ; (1, 3) surg+.

es = more than one (N.);
church+, peach+, potato+, tomato+, bench+.

esque = like (A.);
arab+, burl+, grot+, pictur+, statu+.

ess — a female who (N.);
   instructr+, adventur+, patron+, seamstr+.

est = most (A.);
   bright+, gay+, hard+, kind+, strong+, sweet+.

et = small (N.);
   brack+, lock+, pock+, sock+, tick+, trink+.

ette = small (N.);
   brun+, egr+, gaz+, pal+, vinaigr+.

ful — (1) full (N.); (2) full of (A.);
   (1) mouth+, hand+, cup+; (2) beauti+, cheer+, youth+.

fy = to make (V.);
   beauti+, glori+, forti+, paci+, ampli+.

hood — (1) state or condition of being; (2) office of (N.);
   (1) child+, brother+, man+; (2) priest+.

ian = (1) one who (N.); (2) pertaining to (A.);
   (1, 2) Christ+; (1) guard+; (2) Columb+. equestr+.

ible = capable of being (A.);
   cred+, fall+, comprehens+, access+, express+, vis+.

ic = (1) one who; (2) that which (N.); (3) pertaining to (A.);
   (1) crit+; (2) mus+, top+; (3) histor+, telegraph+.

ical = pertaining to (A.);
   geograph+, med+, polit+, cler+, academ+.

ice = (1) one who; (2) that which; (3) quality of being (N.);
   (1) accompl+; (2) benef+, not+; (3) mal+, coward+.

id = having the quality of (A.),
   ac+, frig+, gel+, sol+, plac+, tim+, flu+.

ier = one who (N.);
   cash+, cloth+, cour+, hos+, prem+, sold+.

ile = (1) capable of being; (2) like (A.);
   (1) doc+, duct+, frag+, tract+; (2) text+, volat+.

ine = having the quality of (A.);
   alkal+, sacchar+, sal+, adamant+.

ing = continuance of action (V.);
   call+, bind+, hold+, sing+, jump+, fly+.

ion = (1) that which; (2) act of (N.);
   (1) confess+, deduct+; (2) divis+, subtract+, vis+.

ise – to cause (V.) ;
  advert+, comprom+, disfranch+.

ish = (1) like; (2) somewhat (A.); (3) to make (V.);
  (1) boy+, child+, girl+, prud+ ; (2) black+, yellow+ ;
  (3) publ+, pol+.

ism – (1) the practice of; (2) state of being (N.);
  (1) American+ ; (2) hero+, magnet+, heathen+, ostrac+.

ist = one who (N.);
  Bapt+, special+, drugg+, pian+, journal+.

ite = (1) one who; (2) that which (N.);
  (1) anchor+, hypocr+, favor+ ; (2) perquis+, requis+.

ity = state of being (N.);
  Christian+, felic+, fluid+, profund+, rapid+.

ive = having the power or quality of (A.);
  act+, destruct+, effect+, correct+, protect+.

ix = a female who (N.);
  administratr+, executr+, prosecutr+, testatr+.

ize = (1) to make ; (2) to give (V.);
  (1) aggrand+, familiar+, steril+ ; (2) bapt+, character+.

kin = small (N.) ;
  bod+, nap+, pip+, fir+.

le = (1) repeatedly ; (2) slightly (V.);
  (1) dabb+, dribb+, grapp+ ; (2) jost+, spark+.

less = without (A.) ;
  end+, friend+, ground+, regard+, home+.

let = small (N.) ;
  brace+, eye+, brook+, in+, pal+, ring+.

ling = small (N.) ;
  gos+, ink+, nest+, dar+, sap+, twink+.

ly = like; manner (Ad.) ;
  man+, woman+, ghast+, open+, rough+, wrong+.

ment = (1) that which; (2) state or condition of being;
    (3) act of (N.);
  (1) frag+, nutri+ ; (2) astonish+ ; (2, 3) debase+.

ness = state or quality of being (N.);
  good+, great+, natural+, light+, heavi+.

oon – large (N.);
  ball+, drag+, sal+, cart+.

or – (1) one who; (2) that which; (3) place where (N.);
  (1) auth+, govern+; (2) elevat+; (3) parl+, harb+.

ory = (1) place where (N.); (2) having the power; (3) relating to (A.);
  (1) audit+, dormit+; (2) compuls+; (3) prefat+.

ose = full of (A.);
  adip+, mor+, comat+, verb+.

ot – one who (N.);
  big+, patri+, idi+, zeal+.

ous – containing (A.);
  gelatin+, resin+, poison+, glutin+, venom+.

ple – fold (A.);
  sim+, tri+, quadru+, quintu+.

r – (1) one who; (2) that which (N.); (3) more (A.);
  (1) appraise+, advertise+; (2) cleave+, typewrite+; (3)
  pure+, ripe+.

ry – (1) place where; (2) collection of; (3) art of (N.);
  (1) grape+, nurse+; (2) infant+, gent+; (3) chemist+.

s – more than one (N.);
  day+, fig+, grape+, hand+, key+, pen+, play+.

ship – (1) office of; (2) state of (N.);
  (1) clerk+, guardian+, editor+; (2) survivor+, rival+.

sion – (1) that which; (2) act of (N.);
  (1) dimen+, pen+, occa+; (2) dismis+, infu+, percus+.

some – having the quality of (A.);
  game+, win+, toil+, weari+, lone+, glad+.

st – most (A.);
  choice+, dense+, fine+, handsome+, sure+.

ster – (1) one who; (2) that which (N.);
  (1) huck+, song+, young+; (2) road+, hol+.

teen = plus ten (A.);
  four+, six+, seven+, eigh+, nine+.

tion = (1) that which; (2) act of (N.);
  (1) decora+, obstruc+; (2) cultiva+, emigra+, propaga+.

tude = (1) condition; (2) position;
(1) beati+, grati+ ; (2) alti+, lati+, longi+.

ty = (1) state of being (N.); (2) ten times (A.);
(1) frail+, loyal+, satie+ ; (2) six+, seven+, nine+.

ulous = state of being (A.);
pop+, cred+, neb+, fab+, ridic+, scrof+.

und = full of (A.);
joc+, morib+, rubic+.

ure = (1) that which; (2) state of being; (3) act of (N.);
(1) meas+, pleas+ ; (2) mixt+, moist+ ; (3) press+, capt+.

wright = a workman (N.);
ship+, wheel+, wagon+, mill+.

ward = direction of (Ad.);
back+, down+, home+, up+.

wise = manner (Ad.);
any+, like+, other+, no+.

y = (1) containing; (2) like (A.);
(1) sand+, grass+, moss+ ; (2) fier+, εpong+, glass+.

SYNOPSIS.

able, ible, ile = capable of being.

ac, an, ary, ian, ic, ical = pertaining to.

ac, an, ant, ar, ard, ary, ate, atic, eer, ent, er, ess, ian, ic, ice, ier, ist, ite, or, ot, r, ster = one who.

aceous, acious = having the nature of.

acy, ance, ant, dom, hood, ism, ity, ment, ness, ship, ty, ulous, ure, y = state of being.

acy, ence, ency, ice, ness = quality of being.

age, ant, ar, ary, ate, ence, ency, ent, er, ic, ice, ion, ite, ment, or, r, sion, ster, tion, ure = that which.

age, dom, ence, hood, ment = condition of being.

age, ery, ry = collection of.

al, atic, ern = belonging to.

ance, ate, ion, ment, sion, tion, ure = act of.

7

ar, ory – relating to.
ar, esque, ile, ish, ly, y – like.
ary, ence, ency, ern, ery, or, ory, ry = place where.
ate, ion, ment, tion, ure = act of.
cle, cule, en, et, ette, kin, let, ling – small.
d, ed – past time.
en, fy, ise, ish, ize = to make.
ency, ship, hood – office of.
ent, id, ine, ive, some = having the quality of.
er, r = more.
ery, ry – art of.
es, s – more than one.
ess, ix – a female who.
est, st – most.
ful, ose, und = full of.
on, oon = large.

PROOF READER'S MARKS.
INCORRECT PROOF,

with Proof Reader's marks on the margin, indicating the corrections to be made:

ac ∧ cent	$\mid \acute{v}$
apostrophe; as in Johns hat	$\mid \grave{v}$
broken type	$\mid \times$
∠ carry to the left	$\mid \angle$
7 carry to the right	$\mid 7$
elevate ⎕ letter or ⌐word⌐	$\mid \sqcap$
∧ indent for a new paragraph	$\mid \square \mid \mathscr{C}ap.$
Italic type	$\mid \mathscr{Ital}.$

~~let it stand.~~ (It is right.)   /stet

lower ⌐ letter or a ⌐word⌐   / ⊔ / ⊔

make a new paragraph   / Cap. / ¶

morespace   / #
    ∧

n͡o space   / ⊂

Out. See copy for that which is omitted.   / out, c. o.

period   / ⊙
      ∧

print æ together in Cæsar   / æ

projecting ▬ quadrat; press it down or take it out   / ⊥

query : Is centre spelled right?   / ?

quotation marks; ∧Truth is mighty∧   / "/ / "/

run in
⌐Do not make a new paragraph   / ↶ ¶

small Letters (lower Case)   / l. c.

take outt; omit this   / ⧸

transpo⌐es⌐; put⌐there⌐this∧   / tr.

turn a reversep letter   / ⧸

    put this even with the other lines .   /

straighten this crooked line   /≡

wrong font (wrong kind of type)   .   / wf.

wrong lʌtter   / •

wrong omission of a leter   / ⧸
      ∧

NOTE.—One score under a letter or word means italic type; two
scores, small capitals; three scores, large capitals.

RULES FOR SPELLING.

The following rules will assist the student in the formation of many words.

(1) A monosyllable ending with a single consonant (except *h* and *x*), preceded by a single vowel, doubles the final consonant before a suffix beginning with a vowel; as, *blot + ed = blotted, plan + ed = planned, run + ing = running.*

Words of more than one syllable, if accented on the last syllable, are included under the above rule, except when the addition of the suffix changes the position of the accent; as, *admit' + ance = admit'tance, confer' + ed = confer'red, confer' + ence = con'ference.*

Exceptions: *chagrin' + ed = chagrin'ed, infer' + able = infer'able.*

(2) Words ending with a double consonant retain both consonants when receiving a suffix; as, *ebb + ing = ebbing, will + ful = willful, drill + ed = drilled.*

NOTE 1.—To avoid a triple consonant one *l* is dropped from derivative words formed by the addition of the suffix *ly* to primitive words ending in *ll*; as, *full + ly = fully, squall + ly = squally.*

NOTE 2.—*All* and *full* when used as parts of a word usually drop one *l*; as, *all + ways = always, faith + full = faithful, full + fill = fulfill.*

Exceptions: *carry + all = carryall, full + ness = fullness, full + grown = full-grown.*

(3) Words ending with a silent *e* usually omit it before a suffix beginning with a vowel; as, *move + ed = moved, trouble + ing = troubling.*

Exceptions: *dye + ing = dyeing* (coloring), to distinguish this word from *die + ing = dying* (expiring); and *singe + ing = singeing* (scorching), to distinguish it from *sing + ing = singing* (melody).

(4) Words usually retain the silent *e* before a suffix beginning with a consonant; as, *trouble + some = troublesome, store + house = storehouse, white + ness = whiteness.*

Exceptions: *abridge + ment = abridgment, acknowledge + ment = acknowledgment, lodge + ment = lodgment, judge + ment = judgment.*

(5) Words ending with *e* preceded by *c* or *g* retain the *e* before a suffix beginning with *a* or *o*, to preserve the soft sound of *c* or *g*; as, *courage + ous = courageous, notice + able = noticeable*, etc.

(6) Words ending with *ie* change the *ie* to *y* before the suffix *ing*; as, *die + ing = dying, tie + ing = tying*.

(7) Words of more than one syllable ending with *y* preceded by a consonant usually change the *y* into *i* before a suffix; as, *busy ⊢ ly = busily, glory + ous = glorious, study + es = studies*.

Exceptions: Final *y* is sometimes changed to *e* instead of *i*; as, *bounty + ous = bounteous, plenty + ous = plenteous*, etc.

Derivatives formed by adding the suffix *ship* retain the *y*: *lady + ship = ladyship, surety + ship = suretyship*. *Y* is also retained in the possessive case singular of nouns; as, *Mary's, lady's*.

(8) Words ending in *y* preceded by a vowel usually retain the *y* unchanged before a suffix; as, *convey + ing = conveying, pay + able = payable, survey + or = surveyor*.

Exceptions: *day + ly = daily, pay + ed = paid*, etc.

(9) Words ending in *c* hard add *k* before suffixes beginning with *e*, *i*, or *y*, to preserve the hard sound of *c*; as, *traffic + ing = trafficking, physic + ed = physicked, zinc + y = zincky*.

LaVergne, TN USA
08 April 2010
178573LV00002B/8/A